The front cover was
inspired by the following
quote from Carlson (1979, p. 52).

"Before we made the study, I always thought of a chief executive as the conductor of an orchestra, standing aloof on his platform. Now I am in some respects inclined to see him as the puppet in a puppet-show with hundreds of people pulling the strings and forcing him to act in one way or another."

SPORT
MANAGEMENT
MACRO
PERSPECTIVES

P. Chelladurai
Faculty of Physical Education
University of Western Ontario

Foreword by
Earle F. Zeigler
University of Western Ontario

SPORTS DYNAMICS
2328 Foul Bay Road
Victoria B.C.
Canada
V8R 5A9
Tel.: (604) 595-2206

102 Anderida Road
Eastbourne, East Sussex
England
BN22 0QD
Tel.: 0323 508676

Canadian Cataloguing in Publication Data

Chelladurai, P.
    Sport Management

    Includes index
    ISBN 0-9691619-2-1

    1. Sports - Organization and Administration.
    I. Title.
    GV713.C48 1985   796'.06'9   C85-099308-3
                        49297

Copyright © 1985 by **Sports Dynamics**

TABLE OF CONTENTS

To the women in my life:

> Sornammal, my mother,
> Kanagammal, my mother-in-law, and
> Ponnuthai, my wife

In appreciation for their strength, love, and encouragement.

Acknowledgments

It is conventional for authors to acknowledge all those who have helped in the preparation of their work. I would like to go beyond that and expess my gratitude to two individuals who have contributed greatly to my professional growth — Professor Earle F. Zeigler and Professor Albert V. Carron. They, in their own unique and inimitable ways, have shown me what I, as a professional educator and researcher, should do and how. Their expression of faith, their constant encouragement, and their positive feedback have greatly contributed to my advancement in the field. But, of course, they are not responsible for the weaknesses in this text and/or my viewpoints. One can only take the horse to water!

I would also like to express my indebtedness to the Faculty of Physical Education, University of Western Ontario. Apart from it being the anchor of my livelihood, it has provided a climate which is both pleasant, and conducive to academic pursuits.

My thanks are also due to my friend and colleague, Terry Haggerty, who has read most of the manuscript. His suggestions and comments were most helpful.

Finally, the Leave Fellowship granted by the Social Sciences and Humanities Research Council of Canada is gratefully acknowledged. Without that assistance, I would not have found time to write this text.

Preface

As a student and teacher of sport management, I have been frustrated over the lack of a text that delved into the macro issues in sport management —issues relating to the nature of sport organizations and their products, the clarity of goals, differentiation and integration of organizational activities, and so on. I had, in the past, prescribed a number of readings for my students drawn from literature in other fields to supplement my lectures. This book is an attempt to fill that void.

While a number of formats are available to present the ideas contained in this text, I have chosen to highlight the larger (macro) issues in sport management using the traditional and time-honored framework of managerial functions — planning, organizing, leading, and evaluating. In my opinion, this functional (or process) approach provides a sound framework for the study of management and/or organizational analysis.

I have attempted to present the material in such a fashion that it can be used by students (both graduate and undergraduate) and practitioners. Undergraduate students will find the material straight forward and devoid of jargon; and graduate students will find relevant references to more complex material.

The contents of this text is a composite of what I have taught in the undergraduate and graduate courses over the past ten years. What I have been teaching is, of course, a product of my training in both physical education and management science, and my experiences as a teacher/coach. Obviously, my personal biases will be evident in the selection of the theories presented, the references cited, and the positions taken on various issues. From one perspective, such a bias might be a weakness. But, from another perspective, it provides an opportunity for the teachers to bring to their classrooms their own point of view which run counter to those presented in the book. What can better serve the field of sport management?

Finally, I would like to make a request to the readers, as other authors have done. If you find somethings worthwhile in the text, please tell others. When you find deficiencies, which must abound, please tell me.

Foreword

One of life's "professional pleasures" is to be asked to write a foreword for a new text on a subject in which you are yourself most interested. This is especially true when you have great confidence in the background and experience of the person who makes this request. If by chance you also know and respect this individual personally both as a colleague and friend, the pleasure of penning a few words in a foreword is increased even more. However, if additionally you also had a little bit to do with this individual's development since coming to Canada, then you are really thrilled to "witness the birth" of a new and valuable text in the field. Such is the case for me with this volume written by Dr. P. ("Chella") Chelladurai.

Dr. Chelladurai is, in my opinion, unique in the area of sport and physical education management in the world. By that I mean that I do not know of anyone who combines the knowledge, competencies, and skills that he brings to this subject theoretically, along with the on-the-job practical experiences that he has had internationally in several cultures. For example, his several degrees in physical education are supplemented by a doctoral degree in management science, all executed with very high standing. Additionally, he has had a successful experience of more than three decades in our field on two continents. Still further, he has become one of the *two* most prolific people of this decade in publishing in this area in refereed, scholarly journals (the other being Dr. Bonnie Parkhouse of the California State University, Fullerton).

This text itself is "a first" in that it brings into play the author's superior theoretical orientation to help people get ready to manage sport and physical education organizations or units. From my examination of the contents and sample chapters, it is obvious that this sound theoretical orientation has been applied to the discussion of practical, on-the-job considerations. There is no question but that the sources employed are among the best that we have available. Additionally, there are helpful questions for individual and group consideration at the end of each chapter.

Where this text can fit into a professional curriculum depends upon the curriculum planning and the sequence of course made available in this subject-matter area at individual colleges and universities. Here at The University of Western Ontario we have been developing an administration/management specialization within a physical education degree program, and collectively we have reached agreement on a stance that the prospective administrator or manager needs (1) basic course experiences relating to administration/management (taken elsewhere within the University) prior to, or concurrent with, (2) specialized theoretical and practical courses that we have to offer in our Faculty of Physical Education. Further, we believe strongly in a management competency approach in which a variety of laboratory experiences are provided.

As I see it, therefore, this new text by Dr. Chelladurai is admirably suited to provide a sound theoretical orientation to those who would follow sport management as a profession. I commend both Dr. Chelladurai and his work to you most highly.

Earle F. Zeigler,
Ph. D., LL.D., FAAPE
The University of Western Ontario

CHAPTER 1

INTRODUCTION

THE MEANING OF MANAGEMENT

THE FUNCTIONS OF MANAGEMENT
       Planning
       Organizing
       Leading
       Evaluating

THE SKILLS OF MANAGEMENT
       Technical Skill
       Human Skill
       Conceptual Skill

THE ROLES OF A MANAGER
       Interpersonal Roles
       Informational Roles
       Decisional Roles

THE MANAGEMENT PROCESS IN OVERVIEW

THE UNIVERSAL NATURE OF THE MANAGEMENT PROCESS

MANAGEMENT AND ADMINISTRATION

PROLOGUE

SUMMARY

QUESTIONS FOR DISCUSSION

REFERENCES

An indelible mark of civilization has been the pooling and management of human effort (Khandwalla, 1977). That is, the progress of the human race has somehow or other been based on some form of management which has seen that the efforts of a number of people were channelled in specific ways. Numerous examples can be drawn from early history to show the historical contributions of management. Robbins (1976) cited an example from Exodus in the Bible. When Moses was overburdened with administrative and judicial duties, his father-in-law advised that Moses should appoint able men as "rulers of thousands, and rulers of hundreds, rulers of fifty, and rulers of tens ... and it shall be, that every great matter they shall bring unto thee, but every small matter they shall judge: So shall it be easier for thyself, and they shall bear the burden with thee" (Exodus, 18, 17-23). This is, in essence, the institution of a hierarchy and the delegation of authority much touted in modern literature.

The construction of both the Egyptian pyramids and the Great Wall of China which involved the labour of thousands of men over a long period of time are other illustrations of sound management practices by the rulers of these countries and their deputies. And, finally, the ancient empires of China and India are examples of organizations which were managed effectively.

Although the study and practice of management can be traced to earliest times, the intense and thorough investigation, and propagation of the art and science of management began in the early part of the twentieth century. Today almost every university in North America offers programs in Business Administration, and other such specializations. It is also common for many schools/faculties of Physical Education to offer one or more courses in Administration of Physical Education or Sport Administration/Management.

Sport/physical activity has become a dominant feature of North American society, and the number and types of organizations whose major domain of operation is sport and physical activity have multiplied dramatically over the past 25 years. In addition to the traditional concerns associated with the manufacture and retailing of sporting goods, there are a number of other different organizations that deal with sport and physical activity. A sampling of these organizations would include those that offer the use of their facilities and equipment for sport and physical activity (e.g., health clubs), those that schedule activities (e.g., sport pavilions), those that offer instruction in specific activities (e.g., municipal recreation departments), those that organize competitions and promote excellence (e.g., university intercollegiate programs), and those that regulate the affairs of the sport or activity within the province/state, or nation (e.g., Olympic associations). All these organizations whose major domain of operations is sport and physical activity are referred to in this book as *sport organizations*. Correspondingly, the management of these sport organizations is termed *sport management*.

The Meaning of Management

There are numerous definitions of management, but all of them suggest that management is the coordination of the efforts of different people toward a common end. Robbins (1976) defined it as "the universal process of efficiently getting activities completed with and through other people" (p. 15). In elaborating on this concise definition, he noted:

> *A review of the administrative literature lends support to three commonalities for any comprehensive definition of administration. These are goals, limited resources, and people. (p. 15)*

An emphasis on the importance of goals and people dominated the earliest work in the area of management. For example, in 1911, Taylor proposed that all work could be analyzed scientifically and one best way determined for its execution. He also suggested that incentive pay schemes (i.e., basing salary on how much is produced) could be used to ensure that employees followed this one best way. Such an analysis of work entails time and motion studies, and the design of appropriate work stations and equipment. This classical approach to the design of work — which is known as *scientific management* — still pervades business and industry in all developed nations. In the domain of sport/physical activity, teachers and coaches speak of the best way to execute a skill and/or implement a strategy. There is a constant endeavor to design new tools and equipment (e.g., fibre glass poles for vaulting, new rackets made of different materials for tennis and badminton).

In contrast to Taylor's exclusive focus on work, in 1933 Mayo emphasized the need to focus on the human element in the organization. His research led him to suggest that people are not mere cogs in a machine; that the satisfaction of personal needs and desires is a prerequisite to productivity. This swing to the human aspects of management — which is referred to as the *human relations movement* — has contributed greatly to the development of managerial thought. But like the scientific management approach, the human relations movement has been the object of criticism because it also focuses exclusively on only one main element in the management process. Not surprisingly, as Robbins definition would suggest, recent approaches to management emphasize both the work and the people. This approach — which is referred to as the *behavioral movement* — is concerned with work, the people, and the processes that bring them together.[1]

The Functions of Management

A clearer grasp of the concept "management" can be gained by exploring what functions are necessary for managers. That is, in order to get activities efficiently completed, the manager must employ certain processes to carry out different functions. These functions were described by Fayol in 1916 in his book *General and Industrial Management*. Fayol felt that management was comprised of planning, organizing, commanding, coordinating, and controlling. There has been considerable discussion around the functions of management since Fayol presented his original list. As a result, the number and types of functions have undergone changes. From the perspective of modern sport management, four functions are worth emphasizing — *planning, organizing, leading, and evaluating.*[2]

Planning

Planning involves setting the goals for the organization and its members, and specifying the activities (or programs) to achieve those goals. As Robbins (1976) pointed out:

> *Because it bridges the gap from where we are to where we want to be, it is the most basic of the four functions. Further, because planning requires determination in advance of action, decision making occurs throughout the function. However, decision making alone is not planning. (p. 16)*

In the process of planning, the manager needs to identify the constraints within which the organization must operate. For instance, the goals set for the organization and the selected means to achieve them should be within the financial capabilities of the organization, and at the same time be acceptable to the society in which the organization operates. Planning also entails forecasting the future state of affairs. For example, in setting up a private fitness club,

1. The historical evolution of management theory subsumes other approaches like *Administrative Management* and *Operations Research*. These are omitted here for the sake of brevity.

2. A more comprehensive list of managerial functions would include planning, organizing, staffing, directing, coordinating, reporting, budgeting, and so on. Some of these functions can be considered as aspects of the four functions emphasized. For instance, budgeting is one aspect of planning. Staffing can be considered a part of the organizing function. Similarly, coordinating is ensured through the organizing and leading functions. For this reason, and for the reason that the concern in this book is with macro issues in sport management, only the four main functions are dealt with in this text.

the manager/owner must be concerned with not only the current market but also the future potential of the market, and probable trends in the activity preferences of the population.

Once the goals and the means of achieving them have been identified, they must be formally stated in the form of policies, procedures, methods, standards, and rules. The purpose of such formal statements is to outline clearly to the members of the organization what is to be done and how it is to be done. These statements also indicate to clients what is to be expected of the organization and its members.

Consider the example of a head coach of a university football team. He sets the goals for his team in terms of a championship, or certain number of wins. In doing so, constraints such as the finances, the quality of players, and the opposition are taken into account. Further, the means adopted to achieve the goals must be within the rules of the sport, the league and the university, and be consistent with societal expectations. The coach then states these goals and the means to the goals in the form of strategies and tactics to be adopted. The plan may encompass the whole season or even beyond (i.e., a long range plan), or it may pertain to the first few games (i.e., a short range plan).

The total planning process is often subdivided and a specific distinctive label then attached to the various components — policy setting, strategy formulation, and so on. In this text, the general term, planning, is used to cover all of the different components.

Organizing

The second function of management, organizing, involves breaking down the total work specified in the planning process into specific jobs, and then establishing a formal relationship among these jobs, and among the individuals assigned to carry them out. While the planning process specifies what should be done and how, the organizing process elaborates on who should do it.

Organizing is not only concerned with the management of each individual employee but with employees in groups. In every large organization, groups are formally created and designated as separate departments or units. This grouping, or departmentation as it is also called, is a critical component of the organizing process.

After the creation of jobs and units, the task of assigning the right people to do the right job becomes important. All the efforts that have gone into the earlier steps are of no avail if the *staffing* procedures are inefficient or ineffective. In fact, a number of theorists place such great importance on this step that they treat it as a separate function.

Another essential element of the organizing process is the specification of the methods of coordinating the activities of the many individuals involved.

This is achieved by establishing a formal hierarchy of authority which specifies the chain of command within the organization. Every organization (except the very small) is expected to prepare an organizational chart to indicate the relationships among individuals and/or departments within the organization.

In the case of a football coach, there is the necessity to assign the available players to the offensive, defensive, and special teams. Within each team, the appropriate individual must be assigned to each position. Further, each individual must be told what is expected in every situation. The play book which is, in fact, a plan document, also serves as a coordinative mechanism. Another mode of coordination is the development of a hierarchy of authority consisting of the head coach, assistant coaches, speciality coaches, offensive and defensive captains, and the quarterback.

Leading

The third function of management, leading, has been defined as "interpersonal process of influencing members toward organizational goals" (Barrow, 1977, p. 232). While the planning and organizing functions set the stage for the work activities to be carried out, the leading function is concerned with influencing or motivating individual members to carry out their specific assignments efficiently.

In order to be an effective leader, the manager must have a working knowledge of the motivational processes of individuals , their needs and dispositions, as well as the situational elements that facilitate or hinder motivation. Because leading focuses on the interpersonal interaction and reciprocal influence between the manager, the subordinates, and the situation, and because differences among individuals are numerous and complex, it has been suggested that it is the most difficult and critical of the managerial functions. For example, Likert (1967) suggested that "managing the human component is the central and most important task because all else depends on how well it is done" (p. 1).

Going back to the example of a football team, when the coach and his assistants encourage the players individually or in groups toward greater effort, or when they compliment them for good performance, they are engaged in the leading function, i.e., motivation. The various motivational posters in a locker room, and pep talks are examples of the techniques used by coaches as leaders (or motivators).

Evaluating

Finally, a manager must be concerned with assessing the degree to which the organization as a whole, and various units and individuals have accomplished what they set out to do. This, of course, is evaluation. Evaluation provides the manager with the feedback necessary to take corrective actions when organizational performance does not match expectations.

The evaluation process entails a measurement of performance and a comparison of that performance to standards previously set in the planning process. If performance does not meet established standards, one option for the manager is to lower the organizational expectations if they are judged to be unrealistic. On the other hand, it is conceivable that changes in the organizational structure, communication patterns, the type of leadership, and/or the reward systems may result in the desired level of performance. In order to determine the proper course of action, evaluation is essential. Another important point worth emphasizing is that evaluation must be carried out at strategic points from the initiation of a program of activities to the conclusion of those activities.

When the football coach views a game film or scrutinizes the statistics of a game, he is carrying out the evaluating function. The feedback he has gained from his own personal observation, and from the recorded details provides a basis for refining or redesigning the strategies and tactics to be used in future games.

The above discussion of the four managerial processes may lead to an expectation that they are carried out in the sequence in which they have been described. This is far from the truth. Although such sequencing of the managerial processes is possible when a new organization is set up, or when an independent project is initiated, a more realistic view is that these are ongoing processes occurring simultaneously at times and sequentially at other times. It is also important to note that these processes are not independent of each other. For example, the feedback from the evaluation process can affect goal setting (the planning process), the distribution of particular activities to specific individuals (the organizing process), and the leadership behavior (the leading function).

The Skills of Management

The concept of management can be understood not only by looking at the four managerial functions of planning, organizing, leading, and evaluating but also by determining the skills necessary to effectively carry out these functions. This was the approach taken by Katz (1974). He proposed that three main types of skills are necessary for management — *technical, human, and conceptual*. Further, Katz also proposed that each of these skills falls within a three tier hierarchy with technical skills being the most fundamental, followed by human skills, and then by conceptual skills at the top. This three level conceptualization of managerial skills was developed by Katz as a counter to the traditional view that managers are born, not made. Although he originally maintained that all these skills could be developed independently of inborn traits, Katz later modified his position and noted that the conceptual skill could not be easily developed after adolescence.

Technical Skill

According to Katz, technical skills involve "an understanding of and proficiency in a specific kind of activity, particularly one involving methods, procedures or techniques" (p. 91). Katz felt that technical skill is specific to that area of specialization in which the organization is engaged. For example, the technical skills associated with manufacturing tennis rackets may not be relevant to running a fitness club. However, there are some technical skills, that are transferable across organizations. For instance, because every organization must manage its finances efficiently, the skills associated with budgeting and accounting are necessary in any type of organization.

The technical skills required of a manager of a fitness club would include a working knowledge and experience in the use of the equipment (various weight training equipment, bicycle ergometers etc.); an understanding of the physiological effects of exercise, and the relationship between exercise, diet, and body composition; expertise in exercise testing and exercise prescription and so on. The person would also need to be proficient in accounting, legal liability, and other concerns relating to operating a fitness firm.

Human Skill

As the term would suggest, the human skills of managers center around their interactions with people. Katz emphasized this point when he defined human skill as:

> the executive's ability to work effectively as a group member and to build a cooperative effort within the team he leads. As **technical skill** is primarily concerned with working with "things" (processes or physical objects), so **human skill** is primarily concerned with working with people. The skill is demonstrated in the way the individual perceives (and recognizes the perceptions of) his superiors, equals, and subordinates, and in the way he behaves subsequently. (p. 91)

The human skills of a fitness club manager would be reflected in the effective interpersonal interaction with the other employees of the organization (instructors, medical specialists, care takers), and the customers. It can readily be seen that since there is much more variety and variability among human beings than among processes or physical objects, human skill is of a higher order than technical skill.

Conceptual Skill

The highest, most complex skill in the hierarchy is conceptual skill. Katz defined it as:

> the ability to see the enterprise as a whole; it includes recognizing how the various functions of the organization depend on one another, and how changes in any one part affect all the other; and it extends to visualizing the relationship of the individual business to the industry, the community, and the political, social, and economic forces of the nation as a whole. (p. 93)

One implication of this description for the manager of a fitness club is that he/she must be capable of perceiving the organization as a gestalt (whole) and be cognizant of the effects of every managerial decision on the total organization and its various parts (e.g., in the case of a fitness club, a decision to buy more costly equipment may reduce the funds available for part-time help which, in turn, may affect the morale of the full-time employees). Further, it also implies that the manager should be concerned with the relative emphasis to be placed on various goals of the club (e.g., whether to increase the number of customers or enhance the quality of the service to be provided).

Recently, Zeigler (1979) proposed that two more skill categories should be added to the three proposed by Katz (1974) — *conjoined skill* and *personal skill*. Conjoined skills are a mixture of Katz's technical, human, and conceptual skills. Zeigler's inclusion of this as a separate category is meaningful since an effective manager needs to be proficient in all three skills. The category of personal skills refers to the development of efficient ways of managing personal time, organizing and articulating personal thoughts, keeping abreast of current events and innovations, and other attributes that make a good manager.

The Roles of a Manager

The discussion of both the managerial functions and the managerial skills contributes to a picture of the manager as a person who is concerned with and has ample time, scope, and ability to carry out these functions. It also implies that the manager is not likely to be involved in routine and mundane activities. This is far from the truth as a number of researchers have clearly shown (e.g., Carlson, 1979; Guest, 1956; Mintzberg, 1975; Stewart, 1967). The findings from these studies are best summarized by Carlson (1979) who observed:

> Before we made the study, I always thought of a chief executive as the conductor of an orchestra, standing aloof on his platform. Now I am in some respects inclined to see him as the puppet in a puppet-show with

hundreds of people pulling the strings and forcing him to act in one way or another (p. 52).

Mintzberg (1975), whose research is considered to be more definitive than the rest of its kind, concluded that the classical descriptions of managerial jobs are myths.He found for example, that instead of being reflective and systematic planners, managers "work at an unrelenting pace ... their activities are characterized by brevity, and discontinuity, and ... they are strongly oriented to action and dislike reflective activities" (p. 50). He also found that contrary to general impressions, "managerial work involves performing a number of regular duties including ritual and ceremony, negotiations, and processing of soft information that links the organization with its environment" (p. 51). And finally, he found that instead of relying on formal information systems "managers strongly favor the verbal media — namely, telephone calls and meetings" (p. 51).

Rather than adopt the classical descriptions of management, Mintzberg suggested that management could be best described in terms of the roles managers play in their day-to-day activities. Ten managerial roles were identified within three broad categories: interpersonal roles, informational roles, and decisional roles. These are illustrated in Exhibit 1.1.

Exhibit 1.1. The Managerial Roles.

Reproduced with permission from Mintzberg, H. The manager's job: Folklore and fact. Harvard Business Review, 1975, 53, p. 55. Copyright (c) 1975 by the President and Fellows of Harvard College, all rights reserved.

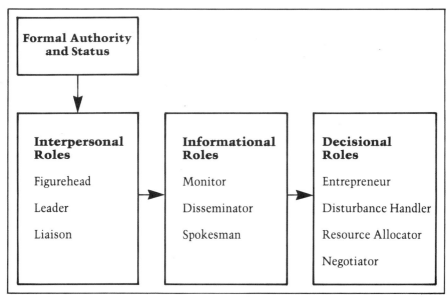

Interpersonal Roles

The formal position of manager involves three different interpersonal roles: *figurehead, leader,* and *liaison.* The figurehead role consists of cere monial duties in which the manager represents the organization in public functions. This role is particularly important in larger organizations. In the leader role, of course, the manager supervises and motivates subordinates while the liaison role involves the establishment and maintenance of contacts outside of the department, unit, or group. An example of the interpersonal role in operation is when the Dean of a Faculty of Physical Education addresses a meeting to honor sportpersons in the community (figurehead); talks to faculty members individually or collectively about the importance of applying for grants (leader); and meets with other deans, the president of the university, and other administrators (liaison).

Informational Roles

The interpersonal contacts emerging from the three interpersonal roles enable managers to become the *nerve-centres* of their group because of the amount of information that flows through them. This informational base leads to three more roles for a manager: *monitor, disseminator,* and *spokesperson.* In the monitor role, the manager consciously seeks information from within the unit as well as from outside of it. The concern in this regard is obtaining any and all kinds of information that will have a bearing on the organization.At this point, the manager passes into a disseminator role as relevant information is passed on to subordinates. The third informational role is that of spokesperson. In this regard, a manager is mainly involved in lobbying for the unit, and justifying what goes on within the unit or the organization. In all contacts with external as well as internal agents, the Dean consciously seeks out information that will affect the Faculty (monitor), conveys the pieces of information to concerned departmental chairpersons and professors (disseminator), and carries out public relations in any external interactions (spokesperson).

Decisional Roles

The interpersonal and informational roles, and the formal authority vested in the position cast the manager in four decision making roles. These are referred to by Mintzberg as *entrepreneur, disturbance handler, resource allocator,* and *negotiator.* As an entrepreneur, the manager is involved in initiating new and innovative projects with a view to enhancing the viability and effectiveness of the organization. It is through the monitor role described above that the manager provides the background information for these new projects. Managers may also be forced to react to changes and pressures beyond their control. Thus, the manager becomes a disturbance handler. Insofar as managers are responsible for the distribution of resources to different units/members, they are cast in the role of a resource allocator. The final role is that of negotiator whereby issues with employees and outsiders are settled. The faculty Dean acts as an entrepreneur when a new program of studies is initiated; as a disturbance handler when faculty workloads are readjusted after the sudden departure of a faculty member; as a resource allocator when budget allotments are made to the departments; and as a negotiator when disputes are resolved. Mintzberg has stated that these roles are inseparable and that every manager needs to be effective in all ten. He acknowledged, however, that "to say that the ten roles form a gestalt is not to say that all managers give equal attention to each role" (p. 59).

The Management Process in Overview

An examination of the ten roles of management and the three skills of management reveals that there is considerable overlap between them and the four functions of management (see Exhibit 1.2). For example, Katz's three managerial skills can easily be synthesized with the four managerial functions. For example, the planning and organizing functions entail a great amount of conceptual skill, while the leading function presupposes higher levels of human skill. Finally, technical skill would be more highly associated with the evaluation phase of management.

Exhibit 1.2. Correspondence of Managerial Functions, Skills and Roles.

Managerial Functions	Managerial Skills	Managerial Roles
Planning	Conceptual	Monitor Disseminator Entrepreneur
Organizing		Disturbance Handler Resource Allocator Negotiator
Leading	Human	Leader
Evaluating	Technical	
		Spokesperson Liaison Figurehead

In a similar vein, there is also considerable overlap between Mintzberg's ten roles and the four managerial functions. For example, a manager's decisions in the roles of an entrepreneur and resource allocator are based on the information gained in the role of a monitor. And, these are, in fact, the essential elements of the planning function. That is, the manager sets the priority of objectives and selects the appropriate means only after securing all the relevant information. Resources are then distributed on the basis of the priority of objectives.

The Universal Nature of the Management Process

Anyone who has had any experience with various organizations as an employee or as a customer/client is aware that organizations differ dramatically from one another in size, complexity, products, objectives, and so on. Thus, it seems to be common sense to state that they cannot be managed in the same way. And yet, the definition of management which was presented earlier —"the universal process of efficiently getting activities completed with and through people" (Robbins, 1976, p. 51) — contains the suggestion that there is indeed a general, transferable process. How can this be?

Simply stated, management in any type of organization consists of planning, organizing, leading, and evaluating; these processes are universal across all organizations. This does not mean, however, that the methods and consequences of any of the four functions do not differ from one organization to another.

For example, the organizing function involves breaking down the total work into specific jobs, and then grouping those jobs into meaningful units/departments. This function is made simpler in smaller organizations with limited activities and fewer members. Thus, a fitness consulting firm with three partners or employees is less complex from an organizational perspective than a physical education faculty with 40 professors and eight programs. The critical point, however, is not whether the organizing function is simple or complicated, but that it is essential in both organizations. The effectiveness of the small fitness consultant firm is as much dependent as the larger faculty on how work is distributed among the members, and how well their activities are controlled and co-ordinated.

From a slightly different perspective, it is also obvious that many organizations which carry out identical programs or produce identical products can be organized differently. For example, many governments are involved in promoting sport and recreation. However, some governments have a separate ministry for sport and recreation; some have placed this unit within the ministry of health, and some others within the ministry of education. Or, as yet another example, considerable differences can be found in the way different universities structure their units responsible for physical education and/or athletics (see Exhibit 4.3, Chapter 4).

What the above examples illustrate is that while the consequences of the organizing process may be different, the process of organizing is universal across all organizations. In short, all four of the managerial functions — planning, organizing, leading, and evaluating — must be carried out if an organization is to be effective. It is only the decisions made under each process that are unique to and contingent upon the specific circumstances of the organization and the manager's orientations. The universality of management across different organizational types is illustrated in Exhibit 1.3. In the subsequent chapters, similarities and differences among sport organizations, and how they facilitate or constrain the managerial processes are elaborated upon.

Exhibit 1.3. The Universal Nature of Management

Organizational Types	MANAGERIAL FUNCTIONS			
	Planning	Organizing	Leading	Evaluating
Business and Industry				
Hospitals				
Military				
Sport Organizations				

Management and Administration

Many writers have made a distinction between management and administration. In some cases this distinction is made on the basis of the goals pursued. When this is the case, management is assumed to be concerned with quantifiable goals and, therefore, is applicable to profit-making organizations. On the other hand, administration is assumed to be concerned with non-quantifiable goals and, consequently, is relevant to non-profit organizations.

Another basis often used for distinguishing between management and administration has been in the general operations of planning and execution. In this regard, administration is perceived to deal with values, policy, and strategy;it is considered to be qualitative and reflective; and, it is assumed to be the domain of the upper echelons of the organizations. Management, on the other hand, is perceived to be concerned with executing the policies set by the administrators; to be quantitative in nature, and, to be the domain of the lower echelons of the organization.

Despite the above arguments, many scholars and institutions use the two terms interchangeably. For instance, the institutions offering courses and programs related to the field of administration and/or management are variously designated as the "School of Business Administration", the "School of Management", the "Faculty of Management Sciences", and so on. Further, reference to the hierarchical levels of administration is made by referring to "top management", "middle management",and so on. Such distinctions imply only differences of degree and not of kind. That is, managers at all levels have to be involved in the same four managerial functions described earlier. But the scope of such involvement in each of the processes may vary from one level to another. Similarly, all managers need to possess the three kinds of skills described by Katz, but to varying degrees. Thus, in this view, the concept of universality of management is extended to the various levels in the hierarchy. Robbins (1976) has argued in favor of treating the two terms — management and administration — synonymously. It is his view that the perceived differences between the two terms are neither consistent, nor significant. Even in the field of sport and physical activity, a number of authors have chosen not to make a distinction between the two terms (e.g., Parkhouse and Ulrich, 1979; Soucie, 1982; Zeigler, 1979; Zeigler and Bowie, 1983). This same approach has been taken in this book.

Prologue

As the table of contents illustrates, this book contains seven chapters. In this first chapter, the concept of management is dealt with from a number of different perspectives: the definition and meaning of the term, the functions or processes of management, the skills associated with management, and the tasks managers actually carry out in their day-to-day operations.

Since the concept of management is meaningful only in the context of organizations, definitions of an organization, and a description of the attributes of an organizations are presented in the second chapter. Also, a number of relevant typologies that can be used to classify different sport organizations into homogeneous groups are discussed.

In subsequent chapters, the managerial functions (planning, organizing, leading, and evaluating) and the problems associated with each are discussed in relation to the different sport organizations. The planning process (which is concerned with identifying organizational purposes and the means toward those purposes) is discussed in the third chapter. The major issue confronting most sport organizations — the ambiguity surrounding organizational goals —is also dealt with in depth in this chapter.

In the fourth chapter (which deals with the process of organizing), the relevance of various theories of organization to sport organizations is outlined. The strengths and weaknesses of various models are highlighted along with modern approaches to organization design.

The next two chapters deal with the process of leading. Since leadership is concerned with influencing members toward organizational goals, an understanding of the patterns of individual motivation is important. Thus, various theories of motivation and their applicability to sport organizations are presented in the fifth chapter. Different leadership theories are discussed in Chapter 6. The major emphasis in this chapter is on showing the relationship of various leadership theories to sport organizations.

The seventh chapter contains an outline of the various theoretical models of organizational effectiveness. Their relevance to various sport organizations is also discussed.

A final note on the contents of this text is appropriate. Since sport management is itself a fledgling field of academic study and research, this book has relied heavily on theories and research from other management specialty areas (e.g., business administration, educational administration). However, several propositions and hypotheses relating to the management of sport organizations are also suggested. Some of these propositions could be the basis for future research and mid-range theorizing as suggested by Parkhouse and Ulrich (1979).

Summary

The chapter contained a description of the concept of management, "the universal process of efficiently getting activities completed with and through other people" (Robbins, 1976; p. 15). The managerial functions, the managerial skills, and the roles of a manager were outlined and discussed. The universal nature of the management functions was stressed.

Questions for Discussion

1. Compare any two sport organizations in terms of the relative importance of the four functions.

2. Select a large sport organization and discuss how, and to what degree the various levels of managers are involved in the four managerial functions.

3. What does the chairperson of your department actually do in a typical day? How is his/her time apportioned over the ten managerial roles described by Mintzberg?

4. Compare the daily activities of the coach of an athletic team to those of the chairperson. Discuss the differences in their roles, and the time they spend on each of the roles.

References

Barrow, J.C. (1977).The variables of leadership: A review and conceptual framework. *Academy of Management Review*, 2, 231-251.

Carlson, S. (1979). *Executive behavior: A study of the workload and the working methods of managing directors.* New York: Arno Press. (original work published in 1951).

Fayol, H. (1949). *General and industrial management.* London: Pitman. First published in French in 1916.

Guest, R.H. (1956). Of time and the foremen. *Personnel, 32,* 478-486.

Katz, R.L. (1974). Skills of an effective administrator. *Harvard Business Review, 52,* 90-102.

Khandwalla, P.N. (1977). *The design of organizations.* New York: Harcourt Brace Jovanvich.

Likert, R. (1967). *The human organization, its management and value.* New York: McGraw-Hill.

Mayo, E. (1933). *The human problems of an industrial civilization.* Cambridge,Mass.: Harvard University Press.

Mintzberg, H. (1975). The manager's job: Folklore and fact. *Harvard Business Review, 53,* 49-61.

Parkhouse, B.L. & Ulrich, D.O. (1979). Sport management as a potential cross-discipline: A paradigm for theoretical application. *Quest, 31,* 264-276.

Robbins, S.P. (1976). *The administrative process; Integrating theory and practice.* Englewood Cliffs, N.J.: Prentice-Hall.

Soucie, D.G. (1982). Management theory and practice. In, E.F. Zeigler (Ed.), *Physical education and sport: An introduction.* Philadelphia: Lea & Febiger.

Stewart, R. (1967). *Managers and their jobs.* New York: McMillan.

Taylor, F.W. (1911). *The principles of scientific management.* New York: Harper & Bros.

Zeigler, E.F. (1979). *Elements of a competency based approach to management development: A preliminary analysis.* Paper read at the Convention of the Canadian Association for Health, Physical Education and Recreation. Winnipeg.

Zeigler, E.F. & Bowie, G.W. (1983). *Management competency development in sport and physical education.* Philadelphia: Lea & Febiger.

CHAPTER 2

ORGANIZATIONS

ATTRIBUTES OF AN ORGANIZATION

ATHLETIC TEAMS AS ORGANIZATIONS

ORGANIZATIONS AS OPEN SYSTEMS
Properties of Organizations as Open Systems
Processes in Organizations as Open Systems
Inputs-Throughputs-Outputs of an Organization
The Systems Approach in Overview

TYPOLOGY OF ORGANIZATIONS
Goods versus Services as Products
Professional versus Consumer Service Organizations
Profit versus Non-Profit Organizations
Private versus Public Sector Organizations
Volunteers in Sport Organizations

SUMMARY

QUESTIONS FOR DISCUSSION

REFERENCES

Management, as defined and described in the first chapter, is relevant only in the context of organizations. Therefore, it is necessary to clarify what is meant by the term organization, its attributes, and its functions in the societal context. Further, since the methods and content of the four functions in the managerial process (i.e., planning, organizing, leading, and evaluating) vary with differences between organizations, it is essential to analyze various organizations in terms of their similarities and dissimilarities. Then, these various organizations can be grouped according to some specific characteristics.

The term organization has been defined by a number of authors. The following three definitions presented by Sofer (1977), Applewhite (1965), and Caplow (1976) are typical:

Purposive bodies which get a payoff from multiple contributions by coordinating them toward a common end. (Sofer, 1977, p. 6)

Two or more people, specialized in the functions each performs working together toward some commom goal, and governed by formal rules of behavior. (Applewhite, 1965, p. 1)

A social system deliberately established to carry out some definite purpose. (Caplow, 1976, p. 3)

All of the definitions for an organization essentially incorporate four elements:

1. More than one person is needed.
2. The members' contributions are specialized.
3. These specialized functions are coordinated.
4. There is a common end/goal that is being sought.

It should also be noted that these elements of an organization overlap with those of management discussed in the previous chapter. This overlap, of course, is logical since the concept of management presupposes and relates only to an organization.

Attributes of an Organization

A clearer understanding of an organization can be gained by probing further into some of its characteristics (attributes). Both Caplow (1976) and Sofer (1977) have listed a number of distinguishing characteristics of organizations including identity, instrumentality, program of activity, membership, clear boundaries, permanency, division of labor, hierarchy of authority, and formal rules and procedures.

Identity. The identity of the organization is separate from those of the members who make up that organization. That is, an organization has its own identity without reference to who are the members and/or office-bearers. The identity of the local Y.M.C.A. is not bound by the identity of the members or the decision-makers.A university athletic department has its own organizational identity independent of its managers, coaches, and/or athletes. In legal parlance, this concept of separate identity is referred to as the "corporate identity". According to Sofer (1977) the corporate identity:

> *helps to separate the personal possessions and obligations of the main body of members from those they acquire in their collective capacity and only in that collective capacity. (p. 3)*

To gain such a legal status, however, an organization must be registered according to the laws of the land.

Instrumentality. An organization is instrumental in achieving goals that are beyond the capacity of the individual members. This is the raison d'etre of an organization. If organizations were not the means to some end, there would not be any need for individuals to join an organization. An individual joins a local sports club because it is instrumental in securing the necessary facilities, in providing expert coaching/instruction, and in bringing together people of similar interests and skills.

A Program of Activity. The notion that an organization is instrumental in achieving certain specific goals also implies that the organization is involved in specific activities. For example, a fitness and tennis club is recognizable by the fact that it provides facilities for physical activities including tennis, it schedules those activities and competitions, and it offers instructions in those activities. On the other hand, a firm retailing sporting goods is involved in the purchase, promotion, and sales of sporting goods. These programs of activities define, in part, the goals of the organization, and the domain in which it operates.

Membership. Organizations tend to define who can have membership. They also establish procedures to replace members who leave for one reason or another. For example, to become a member of a university, one must either have a high academic degree (e.g., a Ph.D.) to be a faculty member, or have a high academic high school record to be a student. This attribute ensures that the organization's members have the skills and expertise to carry out at least some of the activities undertaken by the organization.

Clear Boundaries. An organization's boundaries are defined by the attributes described above. That is, an organization's goals, its program of activity, and its roster of members clarify its boundaries in terms of its area of operation, its personnel, and its customers/clients. For example, a university's boundaries are defined by the activities that are carried out (teaching, research, service), its members (the teachers, support staff), and its clients (the students).

Permanency. Generally speaking, an organization is relatively more permanent than the members who compose it. The Roman Catholic church, government bureaucracies, large industrial and business corporations, universities, and voluntary organizations like the Y.M.C.A. are examples where this attribute is clearly evident. There is a permanence to these organizations which overrides the transfers, resignations, and deaths of individual members. It is conceivable, however, that smaller organizations, particularly those not well established, could collapse with the departure of significant members.

Division of Labor. Division of labor and its consequence, specialization, makes the organization an efficient entity. As noted in the previous chapter, the managerial process of organizing should ensure that the division of labor is rational and consistent with the selected goals and programs of activities, which in turn should make for efficiency. In a faculty of physical education, for example, the division of labor among the faculty members is most likely to be along the lines of teaching of physical activities, teaching of other academic subjects, and research.

Hierarchy of Authority. The coordination of individual members and their tasks requires a scheme in which one or more positions specialize in coordinating the work of others. And, these positions of control and coordination also must have the necessary authority. Thus, an organization is characterized by a hierarchy of authority and a table of organization which specifies who has authority over whom and for what purposes. This obviously results in unequal distribution of power, authority, influence, and status among organizational members. In a faculty of physical education, the dean, the assistant dean, and the chairpersons represent the hierarchy necessary for the control and coordination of the activities of the members. The hierarchy also carries with it the power to schedule the activities (e.g., timetabling), to allocate funds to the various programs, and to monitor activities in general.

Formal Rules and Procedures. A dominant attribute in any organization is the presence of explicit rules and regulations. The purpose of these rules is to ensure that the work performed by individual members is consistent with those standards, and is coordinated with other activities.

In summary then, organizations are characterized by the presence of nine attributes: a separate identity, instrumentality, a program of activities, a roster of members, clear boundaries, permanency, a division of labor, a hierarchy of authority, and formal rules and regulations. These attributes are present to a greater or lesser extent in all organizations. While various organizations — businesses and industries, hospitals, the military, athletic departments, volunteer organizations like the Red Cross, and educational institutions — possess these attributes, some could be quite distinct from others in many respects. For example, the Red Cross and the military are recognized as dissimilar entities since they pursue different goals, carry out different activities, and adopt different internal processes. On the other hand, some organizations like universities and high schools can be very similar to each other since their main purposes and activities are comparable.

Athletic Teams as Organizations

The above description of organizations is broad enough to include athletic teams as well as universities and industrial corporations. Ball (1975) pointed out that while athletic teams possess all the attributes of an organization, they are also unique in terms of the constant roster size of members across teams in the same sport, the codification of the activities of the team in rule books, and the public and precise record of performances of a team. These attributes facilitate organizational analyses of teams, particularly in comparative and cross-cultural contexts.

Organizations as Open Systems

According to Immegart and Pilecki (1973), a system should be thought of as "an entity composed of (1) a number of parts, (2) the relationships of these parts, and (3) the attributes of both the parts and the relationships" (p. 30). Organizations have been viewed by some theorists as open systems. The systems view of organizations is general in nature in that it draws out the basic elements common to all organizations, the relationships among these elements, as well as their interactions with the environment.

The human body provides a good illustration of a system as defined by Immegart and Pilecki. It is composed of different parts (heads, legs, eyes, heart, and so on) which are put together in such a way as to constitute a meaningful whole. Each of the parts has its own attributes or qualities. But what makes the human body a system is the interrelationships among the parts, and the specific qualities which result from these interrelationships. This is clearly illustrated when a short, mesomorphic body type is contrasted with a tall ectomorphic body type. These two specific body types contribute to potential for excellence in specific activities. The contrast between the body types lies not only in the differences in the attributes (parts) but also in the qualities of the relationships among those parts.

A wooden table can also be viewed as a system. Four legs and a top, constructed in a particular way, make up the system of a table. The different configurations in which these parts can be put together make for different systems of tables. In similar ways, almost everything can be conceived of as a system.

There is, however, one fundamental difference between the human body and the table as systems. The human body shivers when exposed to cold, and it perspires in reaction to heat. The human body consumes oxygen from the air it breathes, and disposes of carbon dioxide. These reactions to environmental conditions, and the exchange of energy with the environment do not take place in the case of a table. Thus, the human body can be thought of as an *open system* (relatively open to the influences of the environment it lives in), while the table can be thought of as a *closed system* (relatively impervious to the environment)[1].

Organizations are also open systems since they influence and are influenced by the social, cultural, and economic conditions of the community in which they operate. They depend on society for their resources, and in exchange, they provide some product(s) or service(s) for that society. For example, a university or a college receives the funds and facilities necessary for its survival and growth from the society or government. In return, the university or college provides a service to the society in the form of educating its youth.

Properties of Organizations as Open Systems

The view of organizations as open systems can be further clarified by examining some of the relevant system properties. The two which seem most pertinent here are *boundaries* and *environments*.

Systems, Subsystems, and Boundaries. Every system (except the very

1. The designation of the human body as *relatively open* and the table as *relatively* closed is deliberate. Immegart and Pilecki pointed out that "openness" and "closedness" should be viewed as two ends of a continuum; and that the systems can be located at different points on the continuum. That is, some systems will be relatively more open (or closed) than others. In the above example, environmental influences will have an effect on the table which, as a result, will decay over a period of time. However, when compared to the environmental influences on the human body, the table lies near the "closed" end of the continuum while the body is near the other extreme. Also, Immegart and Pilecki pointed out the possiblity that the subsystems of a system may vary in the degree to which they are open/closed. Thus, the skeletal subsystem is relatively more closed than the circulatory system. Similar differences are likely to be found among the units of an organization.

smallest) has subsystems which can be conceived of as systems in their own right. For example, the circulatory system which is a subsystem of the human body is itself a complete system consisting of the heart, the arteries, the veins, the capillaries in the muscles, the alveoli in the lungs, and so on.

Similarly, a university athletic department consists of the administrators, the support staff, the various teams, and the facilities, and equipment. A team which is a subsystem in the athletic department is also a system in itself from another perspective. It is composed of the coach, the athletes, the team's facilities and equipment, and so on.

While the idea of a system and subsystems is quite direct and clear, the notion of a system boundary is less so. The reason for this is that humans, as analysts/managers must decide on what elements should be included in a system of interest. But, humans are limited in their ability to analyze and manage. Thus, while in one sense, everything is connected to everything else in this world, human analysis leads to the exclusion of a number of things and people remotely related to the system in question. As Khandwalla (1977) stated, "it is because of our ability to fail to see many weak relationships that we are at all able to perceive 'systems' " (p. 224).

A good example of this problem lies in the science of physical education.While all the subsystems of the human body are integrally interrelated, an exercise physiologist tends to focus on the cardiovascular and muscular systems; a scholar in biomechanics emphazises the skeletal and muscular systems, and mechanical laws that govern their action. Each of these scholars has set the boundaries of the system under investigation, but they also acknowledge that their system is integrally linked to a suprasystem — the human body.

In the case of organizations, the boundary of the system is also critical. For a city recreation department, the focal system would consist of all the arenas and playgrounds, the staff, and the participants. On the other hand, for an arena manager, the focal system would be delimited to such things as the building itself, the heating and refrigeration units, the electrical and plumbing arrangements, the employees, and the policies and procedures that regulate the management of the arena. System boundaries, then, are arbitrarily set to suit specific purposes, and anything and everything outside the selected boundaries is considered the focal system's environment.

Environment. In any discussion of the properties of an organization as an open system, it is important to consider the environment. The environment is usually subdivided into two categories: the *proximal environment* and **the** *distal environment* (see Exhibit 2.1). Some of the elements in the environment are more clearly related to the system and influence it more directly. These elements make up what is referred to as the *proximal (or task)* environment.

The other elements constitute the *distal* environment. Thus, for a profit-oriented tennis club, the proximal environment would include its competitors and the attitude of the community in which it operates. The distal environment could include the television coverage of major tournaments which could positively influence the community's attitudes towards tennis. This, in turn, could increase the demand for the club's services.

Exhibit 2.1. Proximal and Distal Environment of a System.

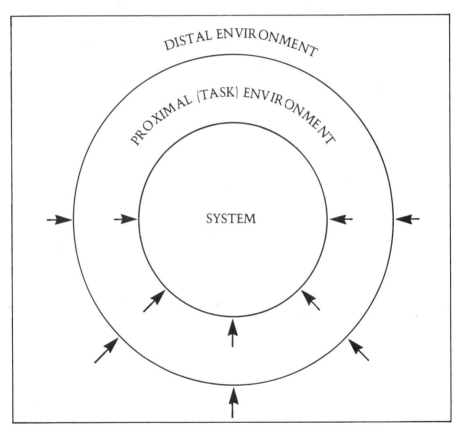

Processes in Organizations as Open Systems

The view of organizations as open systems can also be clarified by examining the processes of systems. The five processes which are particularly pertinent in this regard are negative entropy, self-regulation, progressive segregation, progressive mechanization, and equifinality.

Negative Entropy. Entropy is the tendency of a system toward disorder and decay. However, open systems such as organizations can prolong the length of their life and enhance their quality by constantly evolving and adapting to environmental conditions.Such an attempt to reverse the entropic process is called negative entropy. As Immegart and Pilecki (1973) noted:

> the open system has great control over its existence and destiny; it can choose whether or not to fight entropy or to maximize its existence. All living or open systems exist for a finite period in time space. Few, indeed, have infinite lives. However, the duration and quality of life for the open system is, in large measure, in its own hands. (p. 44-45)

The implication here is that the management of an organization must understand that unless it takes positive steps to adapt to the changing conditions, the entropic process cannot be arrested. Thus, a faculty of physical education must constantly scrutinize its program of activities (e.g., the courses offered) and change or upgrade them to suit the environmental exigencies.

Self-Regulation. The notion that open systems/organizations tend to reverse the process of decay implies that these systems do, in fact, regulate their own activities. Just as the human body sweats to reduce the adverse effects of heat, organizations react to fluctuations and disturbances in their environment. Such self-regulation may consist of changes in personnel, organizational structure, and/or internal processes.

These regulatory adaptations and adjustments maintain the system in a state of dynamic equilibrium. That is, the subsystems of an organization must be in harmony with each other, and the organization as a whole must be in tune with environmental influences and pressures. Thus, changes in the curriculum of a faculty of physical education must be consistent not only with the expertise of the members, but also with the requirements of the society which absorbs the graduates. Subsequent changes in the environment necessitate suitable alterations in the system which, in turn, result in a new state of equilibrium.

Progressive Segregation. One of the regulatory processes of a system is its tendency to subdivide its subsystems into functional and specialized units, and to order them in a hierarchy. Immegart and Pilecki (1973) commented on this process:

> At a basic level, this is the tendency of open systems to determine what subsystems it will formally create, what subsystems it will use to process work, the nature and order of subsystem activity, and the priority of subsystem duties and obligations within the overall system perspective. (pp. 43-44)

The National Sport Organizations (NSO) in Canada offer an excellent example of this process. In response to pressures to improve their operations and produce world class athletes, the NSO created a new subsystem — a cadre of professional administrators each with a specialized function to perform. Subsequently, committees were created to handle elite and mass programs. There was also an ordering of these positions and committees in a hierarchy of authority and responsibility. This progressive segregation provided for greater specialization and regulation of work.

Progressive Mechanization. As the system grows and the number of subsystems with specialized functions increase, the system faces the problem of coordinating all of its activities. Such coordination is achieved by stipulating a set of procedures and regulations for each subsystem relating to what to do, and when and how it should be done. These procedural and regulatory arrangements are developed from the perspective of total system coordination. A large fitness club which offers facilities and instructions in a number of fitness activities (e.g., swimming, weight training, aerobics) would tend to specify rules and procedures for each of the above units so that the total effort would be coordinated and productive. To the extent that these rules and procedures are comprehensive, the task within the units tends to become more and more mechanical and routine.

Equifinality. Any two systems can be distinguished on the basis of the number and nature of their subsystems, and the particular internal processes within each system. But either of the systems can be equally effective because in each system, the subsystems and their processes might be consistent with each other and with the task environments. For example, two football teams might be contrasted on the basis of their coaches' authoritarian versus participative orientation. Both teams could be effective provided that in each team the type of players and their preferences were consistent with the coach's orientation. If players under an authoritarian coach preferred to be told what, when, and how they should do things, then that team would be internally consistent and, therefore, could be effective. Similarly, if the players under the participative coach were more autonomous and preferred to make their own decisions in the course of play, then they would be consistent with their coach's orientation and, thus, could be as effective as the first team. This notion that two systems that initially start from different positions can end up at the same final position is termed equifinality. Immegart and Pillecki (1973), commenting on equifinality, noted:

> This means that open systems have the capacity to achieve identical results from different conditions or by the employment of different processes....This does not mean that a system can do just anything and reach a particular end, but it does mean that given different initial conditions or using different system processes, identical results can be realized as long as system action is rationally, purposively, and causally directed to that goal — provided, of course, the goal is feasible. (p. 42)

In short, the notion of equifinality contributes to the suggestion that there is no one best way to manage an organization. Each organization is unique, and what is important is to ensure that the subsystems and their processes are consistent with each other and with the task requirements.

Inputs-Throughputs-Outputs of an Organization

It was pointed out earlier that an open system is in an exchange relationship with its environment. That is, the system receives the necessary inputs from the environment and processes these inputs into certain outputs for the benefit of the environment. A three stage conceptualization of a system consisting of inputs, throughputs, and outputs is illustrated in Exhibit 2.2.

Exhibit 2.2. The Input-Throughput-Output Model of an Organization

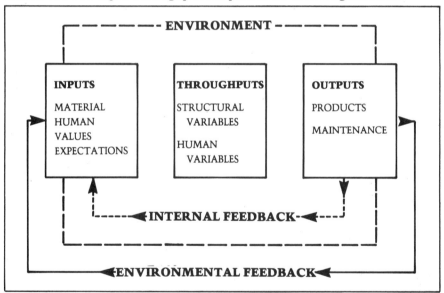

Inputs. The inputs that flow into a system are many and varied. First, the organization needs material resources in the form of money, facilities, equipment, supplies, and raw material. Human resources in the form of professional and non-professional employees are also needed. The personal characteristics of those individuals coming into the organization define, to a large extent, the nature of an organization and set the tone for its operations. Although faculties of physical education in neighboring universities may have identical goals and structures, the way they operate may vary because their professors and students (the inputs) may differ in many respects.

While the organization actively seeks to secure the needed resources, the environment also imposes some demands and expectations on the organization. Societal values, norms, and expectations constrain the organization to operate in specific ways. For example, individual needs and desires are paramount in North American society while group requirements override individual requirements in Japanese society. Accordingly, the structuring of organizations and their managerial processes are different in the two cultures.

Throughputs. The throughputs in a system are all the processes instituted by the organization to convert or transform the inputs into desirable outputs such as goods and/or services. The processes of planning, organizing, leading, and evaluating form part of the throughput. That is, the specification of the means and ways of carrying out the organization's production activities, the structure of authority and control, and the system of rewards within the organization are significant facets of throughput. The essence of good management is to make these throughput processes congruent with the attitudes, beliefs, skills, role orientations, and group affiliations of the employees in the organization. It was already noted that the curriculum design in a faculty of physical education should be consistent with the expertise of the faculty members, the needs of the students, and the requirements of the larger society.

Outputs. The outputs of an organization can be neatly classified as product outputs and maintenance outputs. The products may be in the form of goods (e.g., sporting goods produced by a manufacturing firm) and/or services (e.g., the services provided by a municipal recreation department). It must be noted that the outputs of an organization should be acceptable to the environment. Milstein and Balasco (1973) emphasized this when they pointed out that:

> the system is as dependent upon environmental acceptance of its outputs or products as it is upon environmental resource inputs. In fact, the relationship between the two dependencies — resource needs and output acceptance — is direct, the one affecting the other, with systems thruput processes being the intervening variables. (p. 81)

Thus, a municipal recreation department can get the necessary resources (inputs) from the community only if its recreation services (outputs) are desired and consumed by the public.

Apart from producing goods and services, the organization is also concerned with its own survival and growth. Therefore, the satisfaction of the employees, and the ability of the organization and its members to cope with and adopt to external influences are all critical to the maintenance of the organization, its growth and viability. These aspects, thus, constitute what can be referred to as maintenance outputs.

Feedback. As is illustrated in Exhibit 2.2, there are two feedback loops in the system. One of these is internal to the organization while the other is a channel which connects the organization to the environment. Organizational feedback provides an indication of the degree to which the organization has achieved (or is achieving) its objectives. Any shortfall in the attainment of objectives, and/or deviations from the originally specified patterns of operation would require modifications in the inputs and/or throughputs. One of the concerns of the director of a city recreation department is the efficient operation of the arenas under his/her jurisdiction. Periodic inspections and reports provide the feedback which are the basis for any corrective action taken.

The second feedback loop helps to keep the organizational outputs in tune with the environmental needs. That is, the acceptability of organizational outputs is contingent upon both the quality of the output and the needs of the environment. As the needs of the environment change, so must the organizational outputs. For example, at one time, there was a great demand for physical education teachers. Consequently institutions offering degree programs in physical education emphasized teacher training. Environmental needs changed, however. Thus, the content and structure of many programs also changed.

Another important feature of this environmental feedback loop is that it also provides information on the sources and means to those sources for the much needed inputs. If an organization is not actively seeking information about its boundary conditions and adopting to changes in that sphere, it may not be able to dispense with its products, and, in turn, may not be able to secure its inputs. Thus, the boundary spanning activity becomes critical to the organization. For example, the success of the city recreation department lies in its ability to recruit volunteer and part-time help to run its various programs. It is also dependent upon the department's continued search for information relating to the likes and dislikes of the public regarding the programs offered. Thus, the director of the recreation department and specified individuals within it must be in constant touch with the community.

The Systems Approach in Overview

A systems view of organizations is very useful for conceptually portraying the social, cultural, and economic forces that impinge upon the organization; the people and the interplay of their personal characteristics; the internal processes of authority, control, and task activities; and, the dynamic interactions among all these variables. On the other hand, a systems view is also exceedingly complex. Since there are a number of variables in a system and their interactions are diverse, a systems approach does not permit detailed specifications for the optimal relationships among these variables. Neither does it suggest a managerial approach to a given configuration of system variables.

However, the system approach does provide a framework for the analysis of an organization or a subsystem within it. The manager must, first, define the boundaries of the system of interest by including the relevant elements, and identifying the forces in the task/proximal environment. The throughput processes within the system also must be clearly spelled out. Next any inconsistencies must be identified with a view to correcting the problem or improving the performance of the unit. When any action is taken, the effect of such action on other subsystems and/or the whole system must be examined. Thus, a systems approach emphasizes the gestalt (total) view of the organization while, at the same time, provides opportunities to narrow in on well defined subsystems for the purposes of analysis and action.

Typology of Organizations

A typology or a taxonomy is a scheme to classify phenomena (things, life forms, organizations) based on some relevant and crucial criterion or criteria. It has been argued that "classifying things is perhaps the most fundamental and characteristic activity of the human mind, and underlies all forms of science" (Crowson, 1970, p. 1)

In emphasizing the need for the development of an organizational typology, Mills and Margulies (1980) stated:

> Typologies play an important role in theory development because valid typologies provide a general set of principles for scientifically classifying things or events. What one attempts to do in such endeavors is to generate an analytical tool or instrument, not only as a way of reducing data, but more significantly to stimulate thinking. (p. 255)

The significance of a typology for practicing managers was further highlighted by McKelvy (1975) when he stated:

> Organization science, and especially the application of its findings to the problem of organizations and managers, is not likely to emerge with viable laws and principles until substantial progress is made toward an acceptable taxonomy and classification of organizations. The basic inductive-deductive process of science does not work without the phenomena under investigation being divided into sufficiently homogeneous classes. Managers cannot use the fruits of science unless they first can discover which of all the scientific findings apply to their situation. (p. 523)

Some of the typological systems that are more germane to sports/physical activity organizations are described below.

Goods versus Services as Products

Sasser, Olsen and Wyckoff (1978) have distinguished between a good and a service as follows:

A good is a tangible physical object or product that can be created and used later. A service is intangible and perishable. It is an occurrence or process that is created and used simultaneously. (p. 8)

It should be pointed out that goods may be used in the production of services. For example, an exercise physiologist may use highly sophisticated and expensive equipment to assess an individual's fitness status and then prescribe a suitable exercise program. While the equipment are goods, they have facilitated the service. In other words, the client has not bought the equipment, only the use of them through the exercise physiologist. When a racketball court is rented, the service involved is related to the renting of the court which is an expensive good. Another example is when a baseball glove is purchased in a sport shop. The majority of the cost is for the glove, the good. But, some of the cost is associated with the service rendered by the retailer who purchased the good from the manufacturer and displayed it for the customer's convenience. The difference between the wholesale price and the retail price is the cost of the service to the customer.

Although both goods and services have been involved in some form or another in all of the examples cited above, the service component is the element which should be discussed in more depth because of its relevance to sports/physical activity organizations.

Characteristics of a Service. The nature of a service is best highlighted by examining its pertinent characteristics. The characteristics most frequently discussed are *intangibility, perishability, heterogeneity,* and *simultaneity.*

A service is *intangible* in the sense that the client/customer cannot judge the quality of the product before actually obtaining it. The customer is usually guided by previous experience, or the reputation of the organization, or the person(s) delivering the service. A student's choice of a university could be based on the reputation of the university itself, or of the professors in particular subject areas. It could even be based on the recommendation of a friend. But, the student does not really know how good the service (i.e., the teaching and/or advice) is until it is experienced.

Sasser et al. (1978) have pointed out that intangibility stems from the sensual and psychological benefits that customers derive individually from a service. Insofar as such feelings of comfort, status, and a sense of well-being are individualistic, the services offered will remain intangible.

Services, are also *perishable.* It was noted earlier that a service cannot be produced and stored for future use. If no customer reports to a fitness consultant during a two-hour period, whatever services the consultant could have provided during that period have been lost. Similarly, if a racketball court is not rented, the service (i.e., the use of the court during that period) has vanished. In contrast, a manufacturer can continue to produce goods and inventory them even though there are no sales at any given moment.

Heterogeneity refers to the fact that while goods (e.g., a particular brand of tennis rackets) are usually of uniform quality, services are relatively more variable in quality. There are two reasons for this. First, the quality of the service can be a function of the consumer's psyche. That is, a service may be good or bad depending upon the consumer's frame of mind. Secondly, an employee may not provide the same level of service from one time to another. For example, a tennis instructor's lessons may vary in quality from day to day. Heterogeneity may not be as pronounced in the case of the rental of a tennis court.

Simultaneity refers to the fact that a service has to be consumed as it is produced. When a coach is instructing, the athletes must be present. Because the production and consumption of a service are simultaneous, the interface between the employee (the producer of a service) and the client (the consumer of that service) becomes extremely important. In contrast, the production of tennis rackets is carried out at a different point and time from the customers. Thus, the interface between the producer and consumer of the goods is much less important.

If the criterion of whether an organization is producing goods or services is used, almost all sports/physical activity organizations can be classified as service organizations.[2] (A notable exception would be the organizations which manufacture sporting goods.) Institutions of physical education provide expert teaching in related subjects; athletic programs provide expert coaching to selected athletes; and, intramural programs provide opportunities for participation and competition among the general student population. Professional sport teams provide entertainment for the public. Government agencies such as municipal recreation departments may offer the use of facilities and organized competitions.

Given that sports/physical activity organizations are almost exclusively

2. The term *service organizations* is commonly used to refer to organizations like schools, universities, and hospitals which basically serve the "public" in some form or other. It has been used by Blau and Scott (1960) to refer to one of four classes of organizations based on the criterion of who is the *prime beneficiary* of the organization. They are 1) *mutual-benefit associations* where the members or rank and file participants are the prime beneficiaries (e.g., unions, bridge clubs); 2) *business concerns* where the owners or managers of the organization are the prime beneficiaries; 3) *service organizations* where the clients or the public-in-contact are the prime beneficiaries (e.g., schools, hospitals, sport governing bodies); and 4) *commonweal organizations* where the public-at-large is the prime beneficiary (e.g., prisons). In this text, service organizations are those organizations that produce services as opposed to goods.

service oriented in nature, a large class of organizations — goods manufacturing organizations — are eliminated from analysis for the purposes of this book. But, this does not mean that all service organizations are alike. Certainly, a cursory examination would quickly reveal that the organizations cited above — institutions of physical education, athletic departments, professional sport teams, and so on — are all different. Thus, other classificatory variables (typologies) are necessary in order to subdivide service organizations into homogenous groups.

Professional versus Consumer Service Organizations

The nature of the service provided is defined by what actually transpires in the employee-client interface. For instance, the substance of the coach-athlete interface is instruction, guidance, motivation, and training. Thus, the service provided by the coach is based on knowledge and expertise. In contrast, the service provided by the locker-room attendant does not involve as much knowledge and expertise. Sasser et al. (1978) have used the relative knowledge and expertise involved in the presentation of the service as a critical criterion for the classification of service organizations into *professional service organizations* and *consumer service organizations*.

A professional service organization is a "firm comprised of few nonstandardized branches, offering a broad range of services individualized for each customer and delivered by a relatively high-skill workforce" (Sasser et al., 1978, p. 400). Examples of professional service organizations would include groups of lawyers, engineers, and management consultants. A fitness consulting firm which employs highly trained exercise physiologists would be a professional service organization according to the above criteria. Schools, colleges, and universities would also qualify as professional service organizations in so far as the teachers are professionally oriented. The service the employees provide is largely based on their knowledge and expertise and is nonstandardized in the sense that the service is determined by the needs of each individual customer. From this perspective "the individuals providing the service of the PSO [professional service organization] define the organization, and while employees may be replaceable, every replacement alters the nature of the organization (this is true to a lesser degree in very large PSOs with extensive staffs) and the nature of the product" (Sasser et al., p. 401). Thus, when a professor of sport psychology leaves a university, the course offerings in that field alter, the research thrust also changes, and, in sum, the service product in the area becomes different.

Sasser et al. defined a consumer service organization as one that offers "a limited range of services delivered by a relatively low-skill workforce to a large aggregate market" (p. 400). Most retail services (e.g., grocery stores) and the rental services (e.g., hotels, car rentals) are consumer service organizations.

When a racketball club focuses exclusively on renting its premises by way of membership, it would be deemed a consumer service organization.

The essence of the contrast between the two types of service organizations is in the distinction between two types of employees — professional versus non-professional. According to Hoy and Miskel (1982), professionals are characterized by:

> technical competence acquired through long training; adherence to a set of a professional norms that includes service ideal, objectivity, impersonality, and impartiality; a colleague oriented reference group; autonomy in professional decision making; and self-imposed control based upon knowledge and standards. (pp. 111-112)

These differing characteristics of the professional and consumer service employees would entail different modes for arriving at decisions, organizing work, and using motivation.

Mills and Margulies (1980) have identified seven variables associated with the employee-customer interface that differ among different service organizations: information, decisions, time, problem, transferability, power, and attachment.[3] Since these variables also reflect the distinction between a consumer service organization and a professional service organization, they are elaborated on in the following sections.

Information. The content and nature of information that is processed in the employee-customer interface varies from service organization to service organization. This can be illustrated by the service rendered by a coach and by a locker room attendant. The coach processes many and varied bits of

3. Mills and Margulies have grouped service organizations into three categories based on what takes place in the employee-customer interface and the importance of the information component in that interface. In the *maintenance-interactive* types of organizations, the information processed by the employee is rather limited and the decisions made are simple. This is illustrated by the employee who handles the membership and reservations of a racketball club. Each transaction with a customer involves little time, simple decisions, and minimal information processing. In the *task-interactive* service organizations, there is more time involved, the decisions are more complex, and the employee has more information. As a consequence, the employee also has more power than the customer who knows what is wanted but not how it is to be attained. For example, an entrepreneur, after deciding to build a new racketball-fitness facility, must depend on an engineering/construction firm for a plan and the eventual construction of the facility. The entrepreneur (i.e., the customer) is dependent on the construction firm employee's expertise and knowledge about the specific tasks to be completed. In *personal-interactive* service organizations, the clients/customers are "typically unaware or imprecise about *what* will best serve their interest and *how* to go about remedying a situation" (Mills and Margulies, 1980, p. 264). A fitness consulting firm or an athletic injuries clinic are examples from the field of sport/physical activity. Although the clients/customers may provide detailed information about the source and nature of their ailments, it is the employee who processes all this information and makes decisions. The customers may not be even aware if quality service is being provided. It must be pointed out that the classification schemes proposed by Sasser et al., and Mills and Margulies are conceptually similar. Both use the degree of information processing and the employee's relative level of expertise as the main basis for their respective classificatory schemes. The difference between the two schemes is in the number of points identified on the typology continuum which is used.

information for training and instructing players whereas the locker room attendant only needs to know what the client wants (locker, towel) and whether the client is entitled to it. Thus, the degree to which information is processed and exchanged in the employee-customer interaction is substantially different.

Decisions. Two service organizations can also be distinguished on the basis of the complexity of the decisions made in the production of the service during the employee-customer interface. Thus, the locker room attendant must make very simple decisions while the coach must make relatively more complex decisions.

Time. The time taken to make the decisions will also vary with the amount of information needed to be processed. Again, the coach-locker room attendant example is useful. Coaches, in all of their varied roles require more time in their interactions with athletes than do locker room attendants in their interactions with clients.

Problem. This attribute refers to the extent that the client/customer is aware of the problem and its solution(s). While clients in a locker room know exactly what they want, the clients/athletes in the sport situation might not be aware of the reasons for their poor performances and/or the ways to rectify them.

Transferability. Since locker room attendants are required to make simple and routine decisions, they can easily be replaced, and a newcomer quickly trained. But a coach cannot be replaced without serious interruptions to the team and its progress.

Power. The contrast between employee-customer interface in the coaching and locker room situations is also evident in the perceived power of the two employees. That is, a coach is perceived to have more expertise and, consequently, more power than the athlete. This is not the case with locker room attendants and their clients/customers.

Attachment. The final variable listed by Mills and Margulies was the employee's relative attachment to the organization and the client. Thus, a coach's attachment is typically greater to the athletes than to the organization while a locker room attendant's attachment is often greater to the organization than to the clients.

Mills and Margulies (1980) pointed out that the above variables are closely interrelated to each other, and "are linked to the need for information, the raw material of service organizations" (p.262). Thus, information processing, and the employee's expertise and knowledge become the main basis for classifying service organizations. The other employee-client interface variables might be viewed as derivatives of these two. The differences between a consumer service organization and a professional service organization on the variables suggested by both Sasser et al. and Mills and Margulies are listed in Exhibit 2.3.

Exhibit 2.3. Consumer (CSO) and Professional (PSO) Service Organizations.

Adapted From: Mills and Margulies (1980) and Sasser et al. (1978).

DIMENSIONS	CSO (e.g., Retailers of sporting goods)	PSO (e.g., Fitness consultants)
Information Base	Weak	Strong
Decision Type	Simple	Complex
Interface Duration	Brief	Lengthy
Client's Knowledge	High	Low
Type of Product	Standardized with low knowledge and/or skill	Nonstandard with high knowledge and/or skill
Substitutability of Employees	High	Low
Perceived Power of Employee	Low	High
Type of Employee	Low unskilled operators	Professionally trained, self-motivated individuals
Type of Organizational Structure	Rigid hierarchy Standard procedures Strict control	Unstructured hierarchy Loose control

Profit versus Non-Profit Organizations

The previous section dealt with the classification of service organizations on the basis of the type of service provided (i.e., the amount of information and expertise involved in the service). It is also possible to categorize organizations on the basis of whether their *purpose* is to make a *profit*. An individual business providing fitness services is an example of a profit organization (even if it does not actually make a profit) while a university intramural department offering the same services is an example of a non-profit organization (even if its receipts exceed expenses). Similarly, a professional sports club is a profit-oriented organization while a national sport organization is not. All government agencies are non-profit organizations.

Private versus Public Sector Organizations

The major source of funding has also been used to classify organizations broadly into *private* and *public* organizations. Those organizations that depend on private contributions or capital investments for their operation and survival are categorized as private organizations. Public organizations are those that are funded by tax monies at the national, state or provincial, or municipal level. Thus, all government agencies involved in the promotion of sport and physical activity are public sector organizations. All other sport organizations can be designated as private sector organizations.

A number of authors (e.g., Etzioni, 1973; McGill & Wooten, 1976) have noted the recent emergence of a new class of organizations which they label as *third sector organizations*. The essential feature of a third sector organization is the partnership or collaboration between traditional private and public sector organizations. This partnership usually takes the form of financial support from the public sector with the private sector being charged with the management of the organization toward well defined purposes.

There are two specific ways in which sport organizations may turn out to be third sector organizations. First, the government or its agencies may create a new organization in the third sector. In Canada, for example, the federal government launched *Participaction Canada* for the specific purpose of propagating fitness among the general public. The government provided a block grant of $500,000, and invited certain prominent members of the community including business leaders to carry out the functions outlined. Thereafter, the organization was left to its own devices to promote fitness. The Government's contribution continued to be only monetary, but even that became negligible in comparison to the millions of dollars worth of media advertisement generated by *Participaction Canada*.

The second way for a third sector organization to emerge is when the government begins to provide funds to private sector organizations in support of specific functions. For example, in Canada, the federal and provincial governments in their desire to promote sport have done so by extending financial support to the already existing sport governing bodies. The government's contribution was 20 million dollars in 1983. In the case of some sport governing bodies, the government's contributions amounted to more than 50% of their total revenue. As the contributions from government increase, the sport governing bodies become more and more third sector organizations.

Thus, the distinction between the public, private, and third sector organizations can be narrowed down to the extent to which funding for these organizations is supplied through legislation of a superordinate organization. If this criterion is used, a university athletic department which is financed by student fees on a schedule set and approved by the university senate is similar to a third sector organization. On a higher level, the university itself is, in fact, a third sector organization since it is heavily funded by the government even though it retains autonomy in its management.

In overview, various typologies have been presented for discussion purposes. But, this does not mean that they are independent of each other. The typologies based on profit motive and the sources of funding are not independent of each other. For example, the government (i.e., public) organizations are not profit oriented.Similarly, most of the third sector organizations are non-profit in nature. And, these organizations could be placed on either end of the typology proposed by Sasser et al. For example, a university which is a non-profit, third sector organization is also a professional service organization. On the other hand, a sports arena run by a city is a public, non-profit, and consumer service organization.

Exhibit 2.4. A Framework for Classifying Sport Organizations.

	Consumer Service		**Professional Service**	
	Profit	Non-profit	Profit	Non-profit
Private Sector				
Public Sector				
Third Sector				

The three typologies — the professional service organization versus consumer service organization, the profit versus non-profit, and the public versus private typologies — may be combined to yield a comprehensive framework as illustrated in Exhibit 2.4. But, such a scheme has to await the growth in the number and types of sport organizations and extensive research in this regard[4]. Further, it is not evident if all the twelve cells of Exhibit 2.4 are meaningful in the context of sport organizations. Therefore, in this text, the three typologies are used independently as a frammework to examine sport organizations.

4. In this regard, Fottler (1981) has identified four classes of organizations based on a combination of profit motive and source of funding. These four classes are the private for profit organizations (which are the businesses and corporations whose capital is provided by investors); private non-profit organizations (which are supported by donations, endowments, and government grants); private quasi-public organizations (which are created and partly funded by government, and authorized to provide particular goods or services); and public organizations (whose primary form of financing is taxation).

Volunteers in Sport Organizations

Most of the sport governing bodies and their local units are *voluntary associations*; i.e., organizations run by volunteers. Sills(1972) has defined a voluntary association as

> *an organized group of persons (1) that is formed in order to further some common interest of its members; (2) in which membership is voluntary in the sense that it is neither mandatory nor acquired through birth; and (3) that exists independently of the state. (p. 363)*

This definition is broad enough to include not only sport governing bodies and local sport clubs, but also players' unions and referees' unions. But, the purposes of the unions are to protect the economic welfare of their members whereas the former two — the "truly" volunteer associations — are not concerned with "making a living for the members" as Sills would put it. Further, for an association to be legitimately called voluntary, the volunteers (as opposed to paid staff) must constitute the majority of the participants. For example, the board of governors of a university or a hospital consists of volunteer members. However, the proportion of other paid participants (professors, doctors, or staff) is much larger, and, therefore, these types of institutions lose the true flavor of voluntary associations. In contrast, in sport governing bodies and their local units, almost all activities — top management as well as front-line activities — are run by volunteers. (A recent trend, however, is to insure that more and more paid staff are hired to carry out the ever increasing activities of sport organizations.) The presence of volunteers and their influence on organizational purposes and processes make the management of those organizations sufficiently distinct from the management of other organizations. The differences in the managerial processes are pointed out in subsequent chapters.

Summary

In this chapter, the concept "organization" was defined, and its characteristics were described. Also, the organizations were viewed as open systems, and the attributes and processes of organizations as open systems were discussed. Finally, various typologies to classify organizations into homogeneous groups were presented, and their relevance to sport organizations was pointed out.

Questions for Discussion

1. Describe and contrast two sport organizations from an open systems perspective.

2. The "services" offered by an organization may include the use of "goods" as well. Discuss the degree to which various sport organizations (relative to each other) use goods in producing their services. Also, indicate the relative significance of services and goods within each of the sport organizations.

3. How many of the twelve cells in Exhibit 2.4 can be filled with examples of sport organizations?

References

Applewhite, P.B. (1965). *Organizational behavior.* Englewood Cliffs, N.J.:Prentice-Hall.

Ball, D.W. (1975). A note on method in the sociological study of sport. In: Ball, D.W. & Loy, J.W. (Eds.) *Sport and social order.* Reading, Mass.: Addison-Wesley.

Blau, P.M., & Scott, W.R. (1960). *Formal organizations: A comparative study.* San Francisco: Chandler Publishing Company.

Caplow, T. (1976). *How to run any organization.* New York: Holt, Rinehart, and Winston

Crowson, R.A. (1970). *Classification and biology.* New York: Atherton Press.

Etzioni, A. (1973). The third sector and domestic missions. *Public Administration Review,* July-August, 314-327.

Fottler, M.D. (1981). Is management really generic? *Academy of Management Review,* 6, 1-12.

Hoy, W.K., & Miskel, C.G. (1982). *Educational administration: Theory, research, and practice.* New York: Random House.

Immegart, G.L., & Pilecki, F.J. (1973). *An introduction to systems for the educational administrator.* Reading, Mass.: Addison-Wesley.

Khandwallah, P.N. (1977). *The design of organizations.* New York: Harcourt Brace Jovanavich.

McGill, M.E., & Wooten, L.M. (1976). Management in the third sector. In: Gibson, J.L., Ivancevich, J.M., & Donnelly, J.H. (Eds.) *Readings in organizations: Behavior, structure, processes.* Dallas, Texas: Business Publications.

McKelvy, B. (1975). Guidelines for the empirical classification of organizations. *Administrative Science Quarterly,* 20, 509-525.

Milstein, M.M., & Belasco, J.A. (1973). *Educational administration and the behavioral sciences: A systems perspective.* Boston: Allyn and Bacon.

Mills, P.K., & Margulies, N. (1980). Toward a core typology of service organizations. *Academy of Management Review,* 5, 255-265.

Sasser, W.E., Olsen, R.P., & Wyckoff, D.D. (1978). *Management of service operations.* Rockleigh, N.J.:Allyn and Bacon.

Sills, D.L. (1972). Voluntary Associations: Sociological aspects. In: *International encyclopedia of the social sciences,* (vol. 16). New York: Crowell, Collier and MacMillan, Inc.

Sofer, C. (1977). *Organizations in theory and practice.* New York: Basic Books.

CHAPTER 3

PLANNING

While all of the four managerial functions — planning, organizing, leading, and evaluating — are integrally linked, the planning function must precede the others. This was emphasized by Filley, House and Kerr (1976) when they defined planning as "the specification of means necessary to achieve a prescribed end *before action toward that end takes place"* (p. 429) *(italics added)*. This definition also contains the implicit suggestion that the identification or prescription of an end (i.e., a goal or an objective) is the starting point in the planning process. Steiner (1969) was emphatic on this point when he defined planning as:

> *a process that begins with objectives; defines strategies, policies, and detailed plans to achieve them; which establishes an organization to implement decisions; and includes a review of performance and feedback to introduce a new planning cycle. (p. 7)*

Steps in the Planning Process

Filley et al. (1976) have provided a framework illustrated in Exhibit 3.1 which can be used to help define and discuss the total planning process. In the Filley et al. model, planning is viewed as a seven-stage process comprised of the specification of goals, identification of constraints, generation of alternatives, establishment of performance criteria, evaluation of alternatives, selection of an alternative, and presentation of the plan document.

Specification of Goals

As noted above, the first step in the planning process is to set out the objectives for the organization. Robbins (1976) has suggested that the selected objectives will relate to one or more of the following: profitability, growth, market share, productivity/efficiency, leadership, client satisfaction, and social awareness.

Profitability refers to the fact that a profit oriented sports organization may aim at securing a fixed amount of dollars as its profits. Or, alternately, it

Exhibit 3.1. Steps in the Planning Process
Adapted from: Filley et al. (1976).

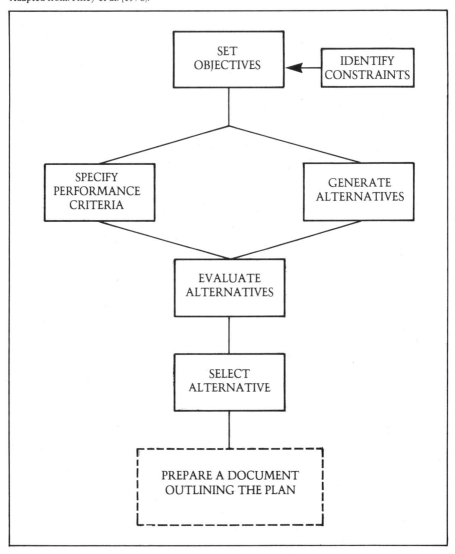

may seek a percentage of its capital outlay as profits. Thus, a fitness firm may aim to make a profit of $10,000 or to get a fifteen per cent return on its capital outlay.

Another objective might be related to *growth* of the organization — growth in term os of profits, total revenue, market share, number of employees, and/or the number of products/activities. The growth concept is equally relevant to both profit and non-profit organizations. For instance, a faculty of physical education may seek to increase its number of faculty members, and the number of courses it offers. Since size is often equated with status, it is not uncommon for non-profit organizations to emphasize growth as their primary objective.

Market Share refers to the fact that some organizations may have the securing of a share of the market as their goal. In fact, relative market share has been used as a measure of effectiveness in many comparative studies of organizations. Even universities tend to have as an objective, the recruitment of a percentage of the total student population.Businesses providing fitness and sports services also compete for a larger percentage of the market in their geographical area.

The concept of *productivity/efficiency* refers to the maximization of the output relative to a given input. Thus, many athletic departments try to insure that a large percentage of their scholarship athletes graduate with a degree. While all organizations are concerned with efficiency, it becomes a singular concern in times of crises. For example, educational institutions have now been forced to consider efficiency in their operations as a result of dwindling financial resources.

Organizations may also endeavor to be *leaders in the market* in terms of the products they produce and/or the methods of production. For example, many computer companies compete to produce new and innovative products (both hardware and software). Also, sporting goods manufacturers compete with each other to introduce new and improved products such as footwear and protective equipment. Universities (and faculties of physical education) also take pride in offering new and more relevant courses or programs.

Client satisfaction also may be an important objective sought by an organization. Such satisfaction is, of course, primarily contingent upon whether the products (goods or services) are of good quality. Rigorous quality control measures, procurement of good quality raw materials, and improvement of production processes are indicative of the concern that sporting goods manufacturers have for this objective. In the case of a fitness club, for instance, the efforts to keep the premises and equipment clean, to provide quick responses to client's requests, and to establish a congenial atmosphere are all aimed at satisfying customers.

Many organizations may also set goals in terms of *social awareness* — being socially responsible and responsive. The voluntary efforts of the chemical industry towards pollution control, and the concerns of municipal recreation departments towards improvement of the safety features in playgrounds are just two examples of social awareness.

Most non-profit organizations are guided by their awareness of societal needs. The Red Cross and the Salvation Army are two examples where social awareness is the main, if not the only, guide for action. Schools and universities are also sensitive to the fact that their contributions are to society as a whole and not just to current students. One of the purposes of any intercollegiate athletic department is to ensure that athletes obtain a quality education so that they can become useful citizens.

It is not necessary nor is it practical for an organization to limit its goal(s) to any one of the above areas. In fact, most organizations have multiple goals. The concept of goals, and the issues related to them are discussed in a later section.

Identification of Constraints

The second stage in the planning process involves identifying the constraints (see Exhibit 3.1 again). While an organization may desire a number of goals, some of them may not be attainable because of the existence of specific constraints. These constraints may be in the form of limited resources —finances, time, or personnel. Thus, for example, a fitness club may wish to expand its program of offerings but be unable to do so because of limited capital. Additional constraints also may be placed on an organization by virtue of societal norms, government regulations, and/or competition from other organizations. Tannenbaum (1950) has classified the constraints placed on organizations into five categories:

1. *Authoritative constraints* — policies of the organization itself can be a constraint. Thus, the university may not permit a particular department to admit graduate students at the doctoral level. Government regulations can also be included in this category.

2. *Biological constraints* — limitations of individuals can render the implementation of a course of action difficult. For example, the lack of a tall player on a basketball team would prohibit the adoption of specific systems of offense and defense.

3. *Physical constraints* — geography, climate, and physical resources can impede the implementation of a plan. For example, a plan for the development of hockey could not be implemented in the tropical countries because of the hot climatic conditions.

4. *Technological constraints* —if the required technology is not available, it can impede the implementation of a particular plan. A fitness firm, for example, may not be able to offer fitness appraisal as one of the services since the available expertise and equipment may not meet the technological standards.

5. *Economic constraints* — monetary constraints can impede the implementation of a decision. Thus, the fitness firm of the previous example may

not have the capital to acquire the required equipment.

A preview of all these constraints by an organization engaged in the planning process would indicate which of the desired goals were within reach, and which were not feasible. Thus, consideration of all the constraints becomes an integral part of the specification of organizational goals.

Generation of Alternatives

After specifying the goals, two sets of activities must be carried out independently: generation of alternative courses of action to achieve the specified goals, and the establishment of criteria to evaluate these alternatives with a view to selecting the best ones (see Exhibit 3.1).

The term "generation" implies that planners are involved in an attempt to develop new and untried alternatives and are not satisfied with simply considering the existing and tried alternatives. Filley et al. (1976) have pointed out that perhaps the greatest danger to effective decision making is "the tendency to ignore the practical difficulty of developing alternatives and to place greater emphasis on goal definition and the process of weighting alternatives" (p. 431). In order to ensure that a variety of alternatives are generated, planners must provide for open communication among relevant members of the organization. Creativity and ingenuity in developing new ways of doing things must be encouraged.

Establishment of Performance Criteria

After alternatives have been generated, it is necessary to select the best one. In order to do so, it is necessary to have guidelines — performance criteria (see Exhibit 3.1). As indicated above, these evaluative criteria must be established independently from the process where the alternatives were generated. Otherwise, there is a tendency to fit the evaluative performance criteria to a preferred alternative(s) and the resultant choice might not be optimal. Performance criteria may pertain to the relative cost and associated benefits of each alternative (i.e., efficiency); to the alternatives' potential contribution to more than one goal; to the alternatives' ease of implementation; to the alternatives' ease of measurement; to the conformity of the alternatives to societal norms and/or government sanctions; to the availability of personnel with requisite ability to implement the alternatives; and/or other similar factors.

Evaluation of Alternatives

The evaluation of alternatives follows the establishment of performance criteria and the generation of alternative courses of action (see Exhibit 3.1). This process might be solely computational in nature if the established performance criteria are all quantitative in nature. Under these circumstances, there is no need for the planners to make any judgmental decisions. However, in most instances the performance and measurement criteria are qualitative in nature. When this is the case, greater care must be taken to be as objective as possible in evaluating each of the alternatives on the selected performance criteria. Any variability in such assessment would falsely indicate one alternative to be superior to the others.

Selection of an Alternative

This last step in the planning process outlined in Exhibit 3.1 is technical and routine in nature. That is, the alternative with the highest rating on the evaluative criteria are selected automatically as the means to a given goal. If two or more alternatives are given the same highest rating, the choice can be made simply by tossing a coin! The simplicity of this step emphasizes the fact that all serious thought, careful deliberations, and necessary computations should have gone into the previous steps of the planning process.

The Plan Document

As a final step in the planning process, the administrators must draw up a document for the benefit of all members of the organization (see Exhibit 3.1 again). This document should specify the goals being sought; the activities to be carried out to achieve those goals; the initiatives of the management in this regard; the corresponding responsibilities of the members and/or units; the standards to be maintained; the methods and measures of performance; and the controls to be exercised at various levels to ensure conformance to the plan.

Rationality in Planning

If all of the steps in Exhibit 3.1 are carefully followed, the planning process is rational. That is, the best means are selected to achieve a given end. It must be noted that the notion of rationality refers to the *selection of the best means* to achieve a goal, and *not to the selection of the goal* itself. Thus, if an individual wishes to own a car primarily as a means of transportation, then the purchase of an inexpensive, efficient model would represent a rational decision. On the other hand, if that same individual purchased a Rolls Royce, the behavior would not be rational. A second individual might wish to achieve status and prestige through car ownership. Thus, if this individual purchased a Rolls Royce, the decision would be rational. In short, the purchase is a means to an end and consequently, purchase of the Rolls Royce may or may not be rational depending on the end (goal) sought. From this perspective, rationality of the planning process hinges more on generating a number of alternatives and evaluating them according to prespecified performance criteria.

Simon (1976) has made a distinction between the "ethical" content of a decision and the "factual" content. The ethical content refers to the decision maker's beliefs of "what ought to be", and thus, it reflects the objective that an administrator may pursue. But, the choice of that objective cannot be proved to be "true" or "false".In the previous example of the purchase of the car, the decision maker's preference to own a car merely as a means of transport versus to own a car for status and prestige cannot be disputed as correct or incorrect. However, the factual content of an economy car or a Rolls Royce can be established as logical or illogical. That is, given the primary objective (transportation versus prestige), it can be demonstrated that the decision to buy one car instead of the other was logical. Simon has also pointed out that the concept of rationality can be strictly applied only to the factual elements of a decision and not to its ethical components.

Planning and Decision Making

Decision making, defined as the process of making a choice from among alternatives, underlies all managerial activities. In fact, Simon (1976) has equated decision making with management. As he pointed out:

The task of "deciding" pervades the entire administrative organization quite as much as does the task of "doing" — indeed, it is integrally tied up with the latter.A general theory of administration must include principles of organization that will insure correct decision-making, just as it must include principles that will insure effective action. (Simon, 1976; p. 1)

The process of decision making is the same as the process of planning. This should not be surprising because planning is one, very critical, area of decision making. Decision making starts with a definition of the goal to be achieved or the problem to be solved. This is followed by the generation of alternative solutions which are evaluated against some prespecified criteria. And, finally, the best alternative is selected.

Although decision making is pervasive in management activities, all decision situations may not elicit the same degree of concern and care in generating and evaluating alternatives. That is, administrators may not attempt to be completely rational in all cases. Concern for rationality in some instances versus indifference to it in other instances provides the basis for two models of decision making: the model of "the economic person" and the model of "the administrative person" (Simon, 1976).

Model of the Economic Person

In the model of the economic person, the decision maker wishes to maximize the benefits and minimize the costs (Simon, 1976). Therefore, all possible alternatives are evaluated and then the best alternative is selected. This is the ideal model of rationality. It is prescriptive in the sense that it details what ought to be done. According to Filley et al. (1976), in the model of an economic person:

> *individuals are assumed to know all alternatives available in a given situation and the consequences of each. It is further assumed that they behave rationally, that is they are able to order their preferences according to their own hierarchies of values, and they always seek to maximize some desired value.(p. 107)*

Although the model of an economic person has an inherent appeal, problems do arise because human capacity is rather limited.Therefore, not all the possible choices will be known, and/or evaluated. Furthermore, the cost of the search for alternatives and their evaluation may exceed the benefits to be derived.

Model of an Administrative Person

The model of the administrative person is descriptive in that it describes how managers actually make decisions (Simon, 1976). Decision makers are inherently limited in terms of their knowledge and capacity to evaluate all possible alternatives. Given such limitations, it is not possible to maximize a decision (as the model of the economic person would suggest). Therefore, the decision maker is prepared to *satisfice* rather than *maximize*. (The term satisfice was coined by Simon from the two words "satisfy" and "suffice". It means that the decision maker is willing to accept an alternative that is minimally sufficient in meeting the goal established.) In the model of the administrative person, a decision maker specifies evaluative criteria that are minimally acceptable. Then, a few alternatives are evaluated against these criteria and the first alternative that meets the criteria is selected. Thus, a decision is made with the least cost of search. The next alternative to come along might have been far superior to the one selected, but the decision maker is not concerned with this possibility. He/she is satisfied with the choice that has been made since it is sufficient for the purpose.

The critical distinction between the economic and administrative models of decision making is that the economic person lists and evaluates all possible alternatives before selecting the best one, whereas the administrative person evaluates the alternatives one at a time and selects the first alternative that is satisfactory/sufficient. According to Simon, the decisions of the administrative person are characterized by "bounded rationality" which he described as follows:

> *The individual can be rational in terms of the organization's goals only to the extent that he is **able** to pursue a course of action, he has a*

*correct conception of the **goal** of the action, and he is correctly **informed** about the conditions surrounding his action. Within the boundaries laid down by these factors his choices are rational-goal oriented. (Simon, 1976, p. 241)*

In short, bounded rationality refers to the fact that a decision maker's lack of ability and/or lack of information sets boundaries around and limits the extent to which a rational decision can be reached.

Simon has also used the term "subjective rationality" (as opposed to "objective rationality") to refer to decisions made with little information about the alternatives and their consequences. In so far as a decision maker has made the best choice with the available information, he/she is said to be rational —but only subjectively. The objectively rational decision — the decision made with all the necessary information available — could prove to be an entirely different one. Thus, in Simon's (1976) view,

*the need for an administrative theory resides in the fact that there **are** practical limits to human rationality, and that these limits are not static, but depend upon the organizational environment in which the individual's decision takes place. The task of administration is so to design this environment that the individual will approach as close as practicable to rationality (judged in terms of the organization's goals) in his decisions. (pp. 240-241)*

It should be apparent that both models of decision making are relevant to management.In situations critical to an organization's growth or survival (i.e., in the planning process), managers must attempt to approach the model of the economic person. In not-so-critical situations such as buying a water cooler for the office, the model of the administrative person is adequate. From this perspective, even "satisficing" (i.e., arriving at something that is sufficient and satisfactory) could be rational if, the decision maker's objective was to minimize the cost of the search and the decision situation was not highly critical to the organization's functioning.

The Implicit Favorite Model

Another model of decision making — the implicit favorite model - was proposed by Soelberg (1967). In this model, while searching for a number of alternatives, the decision maker develops a preference for one alternative early in the search. Soelberg refers to this alternative as the implicit favorite. The subsequent search for alternatives and their evaluation is aimed at confirming the suitability of the implicit favorite. As Filley et al. (1976) noted:

the final decision process is one of decision confirmation. The decision maker will not enter into this period until one of the alternatives discovered thus far can be identified as an implicit favorite. In other words, decision making during the confirmation stage is an exercise in prejudice — in rationalization rather than in rationality. The decision maker ensures during the confirmation phase that the implicit favorite will indeed turn out to be the "right" choice. (p. 122)

Confirmation of the implicit favorite is achieved by selecting evaluative criteria, which when applied to the other alternatives, automatically results in their elimination.

Athletes choosing from among a number of universities that have similar scholarship offers, programs, facilities, and opportunities often adopt an implicit favorite approach. They make a choice early and then examine alternative universities as a means of confirming their initial selection. Similarly, when an organization has a preference for a particular individual and then places an advertisement for the position with job specifications that only the preferred candidate can meet, it is following the implicit favorite model.

Such an approach may be acceptable in some cases where it is used as a counter-measure to externally imposed requirements like a government rule that all job openings in a university must be advertised. However the practice may prove to be detrimental in other cases. The risk of falling into the traps of the implicit favorite model can be avoided if, and only if, the specification of the evaluation criteria is carried out independently of, and concurrently with, the generation and/or search for alternatives.

Planning and Budgeting

Although it is customary to discuss budgeting as a managerial process separate from planning, the two functions are integrally linked. When an objective is identified , and suitable alternatives are selected based on some evaluative criteria, those alternatives must be funded so that they can be carried out. At this point, the allocation of funds to specific activities becomes a simple technical/clerical detail. That is, all of the preliminary steps associated with budgeting have been carried out in the planning process.

Haggerty and Paton (1984) have distinguished between two forms of budgeting: the *incremental approach* and the *rational-comprehensive approach*. In its most basic form, incremental budgeting exists when decision makers look at the total amount of money available and distribute it to various activities, programs, and/or departments based on precedent. This could take the form of a fixed percentage of increase or decrease for every unit based on previous budget(s). Haggerty and Paton (1984) have pointed out that:

the incremental approach does not require much information concerning what programs are actually doing, nor the manner in which budget units spend dollars. Rather, the focus is on percentage (or dollar) increments or decrements from the previous year or historical base.(p. 6) ·

An implication of the incremental approach is that the decision makers are satisfied with the status quo in terms of the objectives sought, the programs instituted to achieve those objectives, and the degree to which those objectives were reached in the previous budget year. It is also conceivable that the decision makers may adopt the incremental budgeting approach in order to avoid conflicts with the units. Thus, the incremental approach to budgeting resembles the planning process although serious thought and discussion have not been invested in the identification of objectives, and the generation and evaluation of alternatives.

The rational-comprehensive budgeting approach forms a marked contrast to the incremental approach. One comprehensive-rational budgeting technique is known as the Planning-Programming-Budgeting System (PPBS). As the name of the technique suggests, it is actually a planning process in a different disguise. The steps involved in PPBS also highlight this fact.

"Planning", in PPBS, involves defining the objectives to be accomplished; "Programming" entails designing various alternative programs to accomplish these objectives; and, "Budgeting" involves funding some of these programs and eliminating others based on the evaluative information on the various programs (Gannon, 1977). Thus, the steps in PPBS are exactly the same as the steps in the planning process outlined earlier. In sum, PPBS and other similar budgetary systems are, in fact,planning techniques. However, some authors find it convenient to deal with budgeting as a separate topic since other related financial issues (like accounting) can also be considered along with budgeting.

In summary, from an organizational point of view, administrators must always attempt to be rational in their planning and other critical decisions. That is, they must try to generate as many alternatives as are feasible, evaluate them on prespecified criteria, and select the best alternative(s) to achieve the desired end(s). In short, they must strive to be rational in their approach. This, however, is not always the case. Two of the factors which limit rationality in the planning process are problems which arise in the organizational goals and problems which arise from a lack of information. Each of these is examined in the two major sections which follow.

Problem of Organizational Goals

An episode from Lewis Carrol's (1969, p. 160) *Alice's adventures in wonderland* is quoted in several management science textbooks to illustrate the significance of goals for an organization:

Alice: "Would you tell me, please, which way I ought to go from here?"

Cat: "That depends a great deal on where you want to get to"

Alice: "I don't much care where —"

Cat: "Then it doesn't matter which way you go."

Goals provide the direction and the source of motivation for the behavior of the organization's members. Goals also determine the standards for performance and evaluation. From the earlier description of the planning process, it would appear that planning cannot proceed without goal specification." Thus, goals and objectives permeate the whole management process, providing an underpinning for planning efforts, direction, motivation, and control" (Richards, 1978; pp. 8-9]. Given the importance of goals in organizational activities, it is beneficial to examine some of the issues raised about goals/objectives[1] in the management literature.

Goals as a Chain of Means and Ends

Consider for example, the goal of an intercollegiate athletic program which might read as follows:

The prime purpose of intercollegiate athletics is to provide the opportunity for the students with superior athletic ability to compete at an advanced level within the framework of carefully defined educational goals. (Chelladurai and Danylchuk, 1984; p. 34)

The attainment of this overall goal of the intercollegiate program is possible only if the coaches of various teams carry out certain activities such as establishing a good program of training, securing quality equipment, and organizing a schedule of competitions with equal teams. These latter activities, then, form the set of goals for the coaches. But, these goals of the

1. Traditionally, goals and objectives have been considered as distinct layers of organizational purpose. In this view, goals are more global and they possess a longer time frame. Objectives are more specific and short range, and are a necessary step toward the attainment of the goal. In other words, a broader goal is broken down into specific objectives, the attainment of which would ensure the attainment of that goal. Some authors have reversed the hierarchy of goals and objectives and suggested that an objective is a larger and more abstract concept, while a goal is more concrete and specific. For example, Radford (1975) drew a contrast between objectives and goals on the basis of the time frame involved. As is evident from the foregoing, there is confusion in the terminology. Robbins (1976) pointed out that "if there are any differences between goals and objectives they are academic and insignificant for a working knowledge." (p. 128). In this text, Robbins' suggestion is adopted and the two terms are used interchangeably. However, the distinction between a goal and subgoal (or an objective and a subobjective) is maintained to refer to the chain of means-ends relationships.

coaches are only a means to the goals of the larger organization, i.e., the intercollegiate program. Thus, a goal for a lower level is a means for a higher level. Fink, Jenks, and Willits (1983) clarify this notion of a means-ends chain as follows:

> Two characteristics of such means to a final goal are noteworthy. The means themselves constitute ends (goals).... Thus, each major goal of an organization is the beginning of a chain of goals and sub-goals, in which each sub-goal is a means to a larger goal. Second, each sub-goal tends to be more concrete and tangible objective than the related goal. (p. 22)

This view of goals and sub-goals as a chain of means and ends is illustrated in Exhibit 3.2.

Exhibit 3.2. Goals as a Chain of Means and Ends in Intercollegiate Athletics

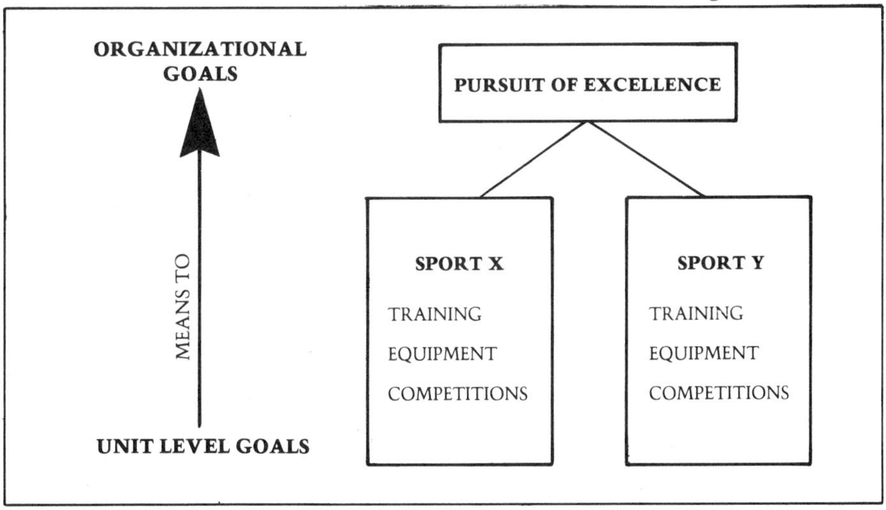

Official and Operative Goals

Perrow (1961) has made a distinction between the *official* goals and the *operative* goals of an organization. Since this distinction is critical to the analysis of any organization, it is elaborated in the following sections.

Official Goals. Perrow (1961) stated that the "Official goals are the general purposes of the organization as put forth in the charter, annual reports, public statements by key executives and other authoritative pronouncements" (p. 855). For example, the type of statement likely to be found in the official pronouncement of a university is "the purpose of intercollegiate athletics is to provide an opportunity for the pursuit of excellence in physical activity." But, as Perrow (1961) pointed out:

> Official goals are purposely vague and general and do not indicate two

major factors which influence organizational behavior: the host of decisions that must be made among alternative ways of achieving official goals, and the priority of multiple goals and the many unofficial goals pursued by groups within the organization. (p. 855)

For example, the global statement of "pursuit of excellence" as the purpose of intercollegiate athletics does not provide any clue as to whether a large number of sports will be fostered or excellence in a few sports will be emphasized.

Genesis of Official Goals. If goals are to provide the direction and motivation for the behavior of the organization and its members, they must be concise, clear, and specific . Further, if there are several goals, they should be consistent with each other in order to provide a unified thrust for the organization (Gannon, 1977). However, in many organizations, the formal goals are stated in vague and global terms. Such global statements are necessary to accommodate the desires and preferences of those associated with the organization, both internally and externally.

From a systems perspective, the organization is in an exchange relationship with the environment. That is, the organization is dependent upon various subgroups in the environment for its inputs and for the disposal of its outputs. In order for such a relationship to continue to exist, the organization must meet the goals that those subgroups hold for the organization. As Hasenfeld (1983) stated:

Human service organizations must also respond to multiple goals assigned or ascribed to them by various publics and constituencies.... An organization may face different publics composed of other human service organizations, interest groups, legislative bodies, and professional associations, all having some stake in the organization and its services. An organization, in turn, may be dependent on these publics for resources, legitimation, and social support, and must, therefore, take their interests into account - interests that may be incompatible or in conflict with each other. (pp. 90-91)

In the case of an intercollegiate athletic program, for example, the alumni, the faculty, the students, other universities, and other sport organizations are some of the "stakeholders" that would expect the organization to pursue specific goals. By the same token, the administrators, the coaches, and the athletes are some of the internal groups with different expectations for the athletic program. If all of these goals are taken together, some may be in conflict with others. For instance, promotion of all sports versus pursuit of excellence in specific sports is an example of conflicting goals sought by two different groups. In so far as an organization cannot alienate any of the groups with conflicting orientations and preferences, it tends to procliam its goals in general and vague terms. As noted before, most of the athletic programs state their goal as "the provision of opportunities for students to pursue excellence in sports". No subgroup can take exception to such a broad and all-encompassing goal statement. Thus, general goal statements are abstractions distilled from the demands of the external and internal environments (Hall, 1972). Warriner (1965) was more emphatic on this point when he noted that formal goal statements are "a fiction produced by an organization to account for, explain, or rationalize its existence to particular audiences rather than as valid and reliable indicators of purpose" (p. 141). Perrow (1961) also suggested that official goals serve the purpose of legitimizing the organization in the societal context, and thus, securing the necessary resources.

Operative Goals. Although the official goals are an attempt to justify the existence of the organization and the support extended to it, they do not provide the focus and direction that the goals are purported to provide. However, broad goal(s) allow the key administrators to emphasize specific subdomains within the broad goal(s). For example, under the rubric of pursuit of excellence, one intercollegiate athletic program may support locally popular sports while another may support international sports. These contrasting orientations and thrusts are the real goals pursued by the organizations. Perrow (1961) called these real goals the *operative goals* and described them as follows:

> *Operative goals designate the ends sought through the actual operating policies of the organization; they tell us what the organization is actually trying to do, regardless of what the official goals say are the aims. (p. 855)*

Reference was already made to two contrasting operative goals in intercollegiate athletics — support of local sports versus support of international sports. If various intercollegiate athletic programs are analyzed, it is possible to identify a number of operative goals. The following nine operative **goals of university athletic programs were identified by Chelladurai, Inglis, and Danylchuk (1984):**

1.*Entertainment: to provide a source of entertainment for the student body, faculty/staff, alumni, and community.*

2.*National Sport Development: to contribute to the national sport development and performance in the international context.*

3.*Financial: to generate revenue for the university.*

4.*Transmission of Culture: to transmit the culture and tradition of the university and community.*

5. *Career Opportunities: to provide those athletic experiences that will increase career opportunities for the athletes.*

6. *Public Relations: to enhance the university-community relations.*

7. *Athletes' Personal Growth: to promote the athletes' personal growth and health (physical, mental, and emotional).*

8. *Prestige: to enhance the prestige of the university.*

9. *Achieved Excellence: to support those athletes performing at a high level of excellence (relative to athletes in other universities).*

Note the following features of the above operative goals. First, all of them are subsumed by the official goal of pursuit of excellence in physical activity. That is each of the above nine operative goals do not in any way violate the general thrust of the official goal. This relationship between the official goal and the operative goals within it is illustrated in Exhibit 3.3.

Exhibit 3.3. Official and Operative Goals

Secondly, while some of the operative goals are complementary to each other, some are in conflict with each other. For example, in so far as providing

Entertainment, enhancing Prestige, creating good Public Relations are all a function of winning teams, they are complementary to each other. That is, an emphasis on any one of the above objectives would result in the enhancement of the other two objectives. On the other hand, Transmission of Culture and National Sport Development may be in conflict with each other. To be more explicit, if Transmission of Culture implies support of locally popular sports (e.g., football), and if National Sport Development suggests support for internationally played sports, then they are obviously in conflict with each other. That is, a greater emphasis on one of these two objectives could entail reduction in the other given that resources are limited. The nature of the complementary and conflicting goals is illustrated in Exhibit 3.4

Exhibit 3.4. Complementary and Conflicting Goals

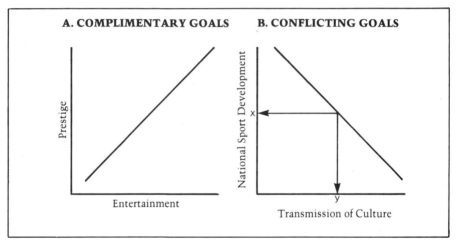

The third feature of operative goals is that decisions on the competing values represented by the goals "influence the nature of the organization, and distinguish it from another with an identical official goal" (Perrow, 1961; p. 856). This was illustrated in a study of the operative goals of intercollegiate athletics in Canadian universities (Chelladurai and Danylchuk, 1984). Using the list of operative goals developed by Chelladurai et al. (1984), Chelladurai and Danylchuk found that those athletic administrators in Canadian universities who emphasized Public Relations, Prestige, Entertainment, National Sport Development and/or Financial objectives tended to favor athletic scholarships, and unrestrained recruitment of athletes.

To elaborate, the objectives of enhancing the image of the university, generating revenue, and satisfying the entertainment needs of the fans can all be achieved, through a winning team. One way of producing the winning team is to recruit the best available talent by offering athletic scholarships and other perks as inducements. (Chelladurai and Danylchuk, 1984; p. 40)

Exhibit 3.5 illustrates the processes that could be adopted by two universities differentially emphasizing the above objectives. It should be apparent from Exhibit 3.5 that the operative goals of the two universities set them apart.

Exhibit 3.5. Educational and Athletic Objectives in Intercollegiate Sports

EDUCATIONAL OBJECTIVE	ATHLETIC OBJECTIVE
▼	▼
Opportunity For Students To Pursue Excellence	**Entertainment & Prestige Of The University**
▼	
Winning is not important	Winning is important
Develop your own players	Recruit players
Treat athletes as the other students	Provide athletic scholarships. Arrange special classes & instructors etc.
Teach them to abide by the spirit and rules of the sport	Teach them the "good fouls" and when to flout the spirit of the sport (e.g. four corner offense in basketball)

Another feature of operative goals is that while the official goals are found in the charter, annual reports, and pronouncements of the top officials of the organization, the operative goals can be inferred only through a scrutiny of the decisions made in key areas like budgeting and personnel.For example, the objectives of entertainment, publicity etc., are not likely to be explicitly stated by any university. On the contrary, many scholars have proscribed such objectives in the educational context. For example, Mathews (1974) emphasized that the success of an intercollegiate athletic program should not be gauged by the prestige it brings to the university, the revenue it generates, or the entertainment it provides.[2] If, however, the actual decisions relating to budget allocations and staffing procedures are analyzed, it would be evident that many universities are pursuing the objectives of entertainment, prestige, and

2. An alternate, but seldom expressed, view of the objectives of intercollegiate athletics was provided by Broyles, and Hay (1979). They were quite explicit in stating that the prime objective of intercollegiate athletic programs is to satisfy the entertainment needs of fans. Starting with this premise, they proceeded to logically outline the processes that would create entertainment value. These processes include recruitment of athletes, athletic scholarships, quality coaching, emphasizing those sports with an entertainment value, and so on.

public relations. Of course, they would never acknowledge this fact.[3] For another example, take the case of a university which proclaims that "all sports are equal". But, when it spends considerable time and effort to recruit and hire a coach at a high salary for one or two selected sports (i.e., it is attempting to maximize) while, for some other sport, it is quick to hire a part-time coach at a nominal salary (i.e., it is satisficing), it is clear that some sports are "more equal" than others.

Genesis of Operative Goals. It has been stated that organizations do not have goals, only the individuals in the organization have goals. This is particularly true in the case of the operative goals which are set by the top administrators of the organization. While the choice of the operative goals are influenced by external agents like the resource providers, clients, and governments, the internal groups and administrators also exercise their influence in the choice of these operative goals. Cyert and March (1963) noted that the conflict over these operative goals leads to the formation of coalitions among groups and/or individuals. According to Hasenfeld (1983)

> *Typically, these negotiations are marked by the emergence of various coalitions whose members can agree on a common set of goals for the organization, and thus can pool their resources to influence the organizational decision making in their direction. The relative power of each coalition is determined by the total amount of resources needed by the organization that it can control and mobilize. The most powerful among them will be the dominant coalition. The negotiations and compromises among the members of the dominant coalition will determine the nature of the organizational [operative] goals. (p. 96)*

A coalition exists when the alumni of a university or college, and the businesses in the local community band together in order to influence the goals and processes of the intercollegiate athletic program. Their dominance over the program is mainly due to the control they exercise over the resources needed by the program and/or the university.

But, this does not mean that the administrators will disregard entirely the preferences of others. Cyert and March pointed out that administrators, and

3. Chelladurai and Danylchuk (1984) argued that Entertainment and Prestige are legitimate objectives for a university athletic program since they benefit the institution and the student body respectively. If universities and their units engage in publicizing their various academic and non-academic programs (e.g., employment rate of students, research grants secured, facilities etc.) with a view to enhancing prestige, intercollegiate athletics can also be used as a vehicle for prestige. Similarly, if universities arrange drama, music festivals, and such other entertainment events, then, it could be argued that intercollegiate athletics, recognized as an integral part of the total educational process, can also be used for the same purposes.

members as well, do respect precedents. In so far as the conflicting orientations have been supported in the past, administrators will likely continue to cater to those orientations. It is also possible to satisfy sequentially the conflicting preferences. (However, in those instances where the organization is blessed with abundant resources the conflicting goals can be simultaneously satisfied). According to Cyert and March, these factors contribute to the relative stability of the operative goals being pursued by the administrators.

The foregoing analysis is best illustrated by the following example.One of the consistent problems faced by a faculty of physical education is whether to emphasize teaching or research. The particular emphasis is normally reflected in factors such as budget allocations and criteria for promotion for faculty members. Slight shifts in the relative emphasis placed on teaching and research occur when there are changes in the top administrators (e.g., the dean of the faculty) and the relative strength of the coalitions made up of researchers and teachers. But, by and large, the functioning of the faculty as a whole is not altered significantly in the short run.

Goals and Constraints

The fact that two conflicting goals cannot be maximally pursued with limited resources has lead Eilon (1971) to suggest that goals may also be perceived as constraints. In Exhibit 3.4, for example, it is apparent that if one objective (e.g., Transmission of Culture) is to be secured to a minimum level (as indicated by point 'x' on the horizontal axis), it acts as a constraint on the other objective (e.g., National Sport Development). That is, National Sport Development cannot be pursued beyond point 'y' on the vertical axis. This notion of one goal acting as a constraint on another is valid only under the condition of limited resources. But, of course, the fact that there are limited resources is one of the main reasons for setting up an organization and emphasizing its management.

Eilon (1971) has pointed out that, from a different perspective, the constraints

> may be regarded as an expression of management's desire to have minimum attainments or levels of performance with respect to various criteria [goals]. **All constraints are, therefore, expressions of goals."** (p. 295).

Thus, when it is stated that a minimum number of women's sports must be supported by the total intercollegiate athletic program, a constraint has been placed on the program, but, also a goal statement has been made by the administration.

In summary, two factors reduce the rationality of the planning process.

First, ambiguity in the statement of official goals (and the inherent instability of the operative goals) do not permit rational planning over a period of time. Second, possible conflicts among the goals of an organization make one goal a constraint on another.

Information and Planning

Another factor that limits the rationality and effectiveness of the planning process is paucity of information. While information (or the lack of it) bears directly on any decision, its impact is more pronounced in forecasting the future, and in generating or developing alternative solutions which are essential steps in the planning process. These two sub-processes of planning require a special type of skill and knowledge base.

Forecasting

Planning, by definition, deals with the future. That is, specific programs or activities are instituted in the expectation that they will lead to some desired outcomes at a future point in time. These expectations are based on some assumptions regarding the state of affairs in the future. Although the future cannot be perfectly predicted, individuals (whether they are administrators or not) do make some assumptions about the future in almost every activity in which they engage. For instance, if children make plans to play soccer the next afternoon, they assume that it will not rain during that time period. Such a forecast may be based on the weather reports, or intuition, or even a belief in luck. Since children's soccer is not a significant spectator event, the presence or absence of rain is relatively unimportant. However, if the event being planned is a World Cup championship three years in the future (i.e., the world championships in soccer), the accuracy of the forecast is critical. In this case, the planners must look into the forecasts, records of rainfall in previous years, the texture and drainage of the playing fields, and their durability in rainy conditions. The forecasts should also include details about economic, political, and social conditions that might prevail at the time of the world championships. All of these factors could affect the successful conduct of the World Cup. Thus, planners must take every effort to gather all available information and tap all possible sources. This, in effect, is forecasting. Gannon (1977) stated that in general,

> the four basic purposes of forecasting are to predict furture **demand** for the organization's goods or services; future **trends** in demand; future **changes** in these trends; and the **magnitude** of change in the trends. (p. 119)

Predicting future trends is not an easy task, however, since trends are merely trends — a point which was highlighted by Chairncross:

A trend is a trend. The question is when will it bend? Will it climb higher and higher, or eventually expire, and come to an untimely end? (quoted in Dessler, 1979; p. 57)

The importance as well as the difficulty of forecasting increases with the planning time frame. That is, forecasting tomorrow's weather is much easier than forecasting the weather two years in advance. Using past trends and present situations to predict tomorrow's conditions is an uncertain enterprise. This has been illustrated by the plight of educational institutions. In all long range plans, enrollment figures must be forecast. These depend on population trends, the job market, and the orientation of new generations toward higher education. History abounds with instances where the forecasts of educational institutes were far from the real occurrences.

Planners can profitably use many of the reports published by government agencies and other private research organizations. There are numerous statistical reports which relate to the Gross National Product (GNP), leading indicators of economic growth, population trends, and so on. Planners may also engage in gathering information by polling relevant individuals. For instance, the director of a city recreation department can poll the residents of the city concerning their preferences for activities or programs for the future. Or, the director can ask the city administrators about future trends in the budgetary allocations for recreation.

Planners may also seek the assistance of experts in the field to help in the formulation of forecasts. Two specific techniques used to capitalize on the skills of experts are the nominal group technique and the Delphi technique.

Nominal Group Technique. In the nominal group technique, approximately eight to ten experts are brought together in a structured format. That is, after receiving the question or the problem of interest, the members are allowed to think about the issue for a short period of time. Following this, each expert must present his/her ideas in consecutive order. After all the experts have presented their ideas, limited interaction is permitted. Following this, each expert ranks the ideas on the basis of the probability of their occurrence. The average of these rankings is then accepted as the forecast for that particular question. In the nominal group technique, it is important that all the ideas are given equal importance. Therefore, a secretary or moderator must be present to not only record all the proceedings but, also to ensure that every idea is given equal time and attention.

Delphi Technique. The general concept underlying the Delphi technique is the same as in the nominal group technique. That is, the opinion of experts is sought individually. But the difference between the two techniques is that in the Delphi technique, the experts do not gather together for a meeting. The anonymity of the participants is crucial for the process.

Typically, a problem such as "Will soccer succeed as a professional sport in North America?" is mailed to experts who respond in writing to indicate their opinions of the future state relating to the question posed. Then, a summary of these opinions is prepared and sent back to each expert. The experts are then allowed to revise their estimates based on this feedback. This total process may be repeated a number of times. Those experts whose estimates deviate from the average are asked to justify their position. A final report summarizing the opinions of the group is then submitted to the top management.

There is some evidence that the nominal group and Delphi techniques are superior to conventional interacting groups (e.g., Van de Ven and Delbecq, 1974). Although they have been primarily used in forecasting technological changes, they could also be used for sport and physical activity management. In fact, Thueson (1985) used this technique to forecast the future of the academic field of sport psychology. He reported that a consensus exists among the experts that the clinical aspects of sport psychology will be emphasized in the future and that more and better courses will be developed with an interdisciplinary orientation.

The Rolling Forecast. Gannon (1977) has suggested that organizations should update their forecast when new information about the future becomes available. An organization might draw up a five-year plan but after a year, new evidence might arise revealing that the earlier forecasts were not accurate. Therefore, a new set of forecasts would be required. Also, of course, plans would have to be redrawn to be consistent with the new forecast.

This is not an unusual scenario. Many organizations actually draw up a three-year or five-year plan, *but they do it every year.* During the periodic planning phases, the original forecasts, budget estimates, and other vital parameters of planning are revised on the basis of new information available to the planners.

Alternative Generation

While forecasting requires expert knowledge about past historical data, their trends, and the future, alternative generation requires innovative ability and creativity. Alternative generation is perhaps the most critical step in planning and, therefore, management must attempt to harness the creative abilities of relevant members during this state of the planning process.

Brainstorming. One technique that has been successfully used in encouraging and marshalling the creativity and ingenuity of members is brainstorming. Osborn (1953), who developed this technique, suggested that the brain is used to storm a creative problem in the same fashion that commandos might audaciously attack an objective. The brainstorming process calls for relevant members to gather together and present their ideas one at a time. A significant guideline of this process is that no one is permitted to evaluate the ideas as they are presented. This enables individuals to come up with a variety of ideas without fear of being ridiculed or criticized. A basic premise in brainstorming is that it is important to encourage a large number of different ideas even if they seem improbable, preposterous, or foolish. In Osborn's view, it is much more difficult to come up with new ideas than it is to evaluate them.

Another crucial aspect of the brainstorming process is that members are allowed to "hitch-hike" on the ideas of others. That is, after hearing another idea, members may be able to improve on it or combine it with two or more ideas to make a better idea. Some members may be better hitch-hikers than originators of ideas and planners must capitalize on both types of talents.

The rationality and effectiveness of the planning process is dependent upon the availability of relevant information. Although the discussion in this section has focussed on forecasting and alternative generation only, the importance of information must not be overlooked in other phases of planning. To the extent that information is lacking, the planning process will not be rational.

Directional Planning

In the conventional view of planning, the first step in the process involves setting specific, concise, and clear goals. McCaskey (1974), however, had proposed another mode of planning whereby

> the planner or planners identify a domain and direction. **Domain** is the area in which the organization or individual will work. The **direction** is the actor's tendencies, the favored styles of perceiving and doing. Instead of specifying concrete, measurable goals, the planners work more from who they are and what they like to do. (p. 283)

McCaskey suggested that in those cases where the organization cannot spell out specific goals, it should set the domain for its activities, and let the organization members move ahead in that domain according to their preferred ways of acting. It is quite conceivable that as the organization moves, it will discover goals.

For example, a private profit-oriented firm might decide that its domain is the fitness area. The proprietor, then would lease some exercise equipment and set up a fitness center. This initial business activity could be based on personal expertise and experience on the part of the proprietor in fitness activities. After a period of time, the proprietor might note that customers were bored with the monotonous and tedious workouts. Based on this observation, the proprietor might open up a few racketball courts with a view to providing variety for the customers. In the course of time, the firm might expand to include a tennis court, a badminton court, a sauna, a pool, and possibly even an area for food and liquor (which are activities unrelated to fitness). In the end, the firm might turn out to be in the recreation business rather than in the fitness business.

Another example is that of a Swiss watch company which started out manufacturing watches for the general public but which ended up producing high-priced watches for the very rich. The chairman of the company was reported to have denied that his company was in the watch business. He insisted that it was in the "luxury" business. The above examples illustrate McCaskey's suggestion that new goals can be discovered and highlighted after the organization begins operating in a domain.

McCaskey emphasized the flexibility that directional planning offers. The specific goals sought are determined only after acting and after interaction with environmental forces —an approach which is consistent with the systems view of organizations (see Chapter 2). Planning in this manner permits planners to capitalize on unexpected opportunities and/or adapt to new constraints which may arise after the organization has entered a domain.

Although McCaskey has advocated a general directional approach to planning (whereby a domain and direction are initially identified), he has also acknowledged that planning with specific goals is appropriate under certain conditions. According to McCaskey, planning with goals is more suitable when: 1) planners want to narrow the focus so that the efforts of members will converge; 2) the environment of the organization is stable and predictable; 3) there are severe time and resources limitations which call for programming of activities; and, 4) members prefer well defined conditions for their work. Similarly, planning without goals (i.e., directional planning) is appropriate when: 1) the organization has just come into existence; 2) the environment is unpredictable; and 3) members cannot build enough trust or agreement to decide on a common goal.

Directional Planning and Official Goals

It should be pointed out that McCaskey's distinction between planning with goals and directional planning (or planning without goals) is conceptually similar to Perrow's (1961) notion of dichotomizing goals into official versus operative goals. Official goals are stated in very broad, general terms, and thus, they serve to outline a general domain for organizational activity.

On the other hand, the choice of operative goals is a reflection of the specific thrust of the organizations at a given point in time. Thus, operative goals may shift with changes in administrators, personnel, and/or environmental conditions. This is directly comparable to the flexibility afforded by directional planning. The overlapping of these two conceptual schemes is illustrated in Exhibit 3.6. In this example, the operative goals are shown to be within the domain agreed upon for intercollegiate athletics. Also, it should be apparent that, although the shifts in focus are drastic, the organizational efforts remain within the general domain.

Exhibit 3.6. Shifts in Operative Goals Within Directional Planning

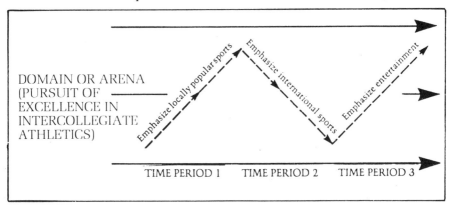

Directional Planning and Information

One of the main reasons why McCaskey advocated directional planning is that planners never have all the necessary information to permit them to be specific about their goals. In directional planning, it is possible to work around the paucity of information, and to proceed and act in the general domain or direction. In the course of time, as new information becomes available, planners can become more specific in their planning.

Planning and Sport Organizations

In the previous sections, a distinction between official and operative goals was made. It was also noted that stating an official goal involves specifying the domain or direction for the organizational activity. It is useful to examine the relevance of these two concepts for various types of sport organizations referred to in Chapter 2.

Private Sector Organizations

Since private, profit oriented organizations are funded by investors whose main interest is to obtain a return on their investment, they are likely to be more specific in their planning than private non-profit organizations. Although profit-oriented organizations, particularly newly established ones, might utilize directional planning, their primary drive for profit would require planning with specific goals. Private non-profit organizations, such as the local

Y.M.C.A., are dependent upon a number of subgroups for their inputs. The demands of their donors and contributors could be in conflict. As a result, shifts in the direction of activities are more likely to occur in the case of non-profit organizations than in the case of profit oriented organizations. Therefore, non-profit organizations are likely to state their goals in global terms in order to encompass all the various orientations. This represents directional planning rather than planning with goals.

Public Sector Organizations

The public sector organizations (i.e., the government agencies involved with sport) are operated on tax monies. Thus, their principal concern is with uniform treatment of all clients/customers and consistency in operations. To fulfill these requirements, the public sector organizations must state their goals in more precise and quantitative terms and clearly identify the activities to be carried out. Very specific procedural guidelines must be established, and strict control mechanisms instituted. From this perspective, public sector organizations must rely on planning with goals rather than on a directional planning approach.

Third Sector Organizations

The third sector organizations represent two contrasting scenarios. First, if the third sector organization is the only one of its kind, the goal statements and planning are likely to be directional. It was pointed out previously that *Participaction Canada* was set up by the Canadian government to enhance fitness awareness among Canadian people. Once this general domain was identified, the organization was left to carry on its activities. The government's only continuing involvement was through a financial contribution. Subsequently, *Participaction Canada* acted on its own, and adapted and evolved according to situational exigencies and opportunities.

If, on the other hand, a number of similar third sector organizations were in existence, the government, as the prime benefactor, would have to be concerned with uniform and consistent operations. Therefore, specific goal statements and identification of appropriate activities, and clear procedural guidelines would become necessary.

Sport organizations responsible for Olympic teams are another case in point. In many countries throughout the world, the federal government is the major (if not sole) financial contributor. But, this financial support is contingent upon the sport governing bodies pursuing certain specific and quantifiable goals, and engaging in specific activities. In fact, in most instances specific guidelines are attached to the contributions. These guidelines set out how much money will be granted and for what kinds of activities. Because the sport governing bodies are dependent on these grants, they must adhere to these guidelines. Consequently, they must plan with goals.

Professional and Consumer Service Organizations

It was pointed out in Chapter 2 that the fundamental difference between a professional service organization and a consumer service organization is in the type of service provided and the degree of information that must be processed to provide that service. It was also pointed out that the professional service organizations and their employees face a relatively more variable and complex environment than the consumer service organizations. Essentially, the services in professional service organizations are aimed at meeting the changing needs of clients. Thus, the services cannot be predetermined. In contrast, the services in consumer service organizations can be standardized and the activities for the employees can be spelled out. That is, it is possible for managers in consumer service organizations to specify the exact procedures and routines for their employees to use. This is not the case in professional service organizations. Furthermore, performance standards can easily be set and monitored in the consumer service organizations; these are relatively more difficult to set out in the professional service organizations. Thus, these contrasting service goals and processes coincide with the distinction between planning with goals and planning without goals. That is, planning with goals is more appropriate for consumer service organizations while directional planning is better suited in the professional service organizations.

Summary

The planning process was defined and the steps in planning were described. The problems associated with planning — the problem of non-specific goals, and the problem of paucity of information — were highlighted. An alternate mode of planning, i.e., planning without goals or directional planning, was described. Finally, the relevance of the two modes of planning to various sport organizations was discussed.

Questions for Discussion

1. Consider a sport organization of your choice. What are the areas in which the decision makers attempt to maximize or "satisfice"?

2. In your opinion, what operative goals are emphasized in your intercollegiate athletic program and/or school? Explain the basis of your opinion.

3. Discuss the environmental factors that influence the goals of your intercollegiate athletic program. Is there a dominant coalition among these factors? How does this coalition achieve dominance over others?

References

Broyles, J.F.,and Hay, R.D. (1979). *Administration of athletic programs: A managerial approach.* Englewood Cliffs, N.J.: Prentice-Hall, Inc.

Carroll, L. (1969). Alice's adventures in wonderland. In: Rackin, D. (Ed.) *Alice's adventures in wonderland: A critical handbook.* Belmont,Ca.: Wadsworth Publishing Company.

Chelladurai, P., and Danylchuk, K.E. (1984). Operative goals of intercollegiate athletics: Perceptions of athletic administrators. *Canadian Journal of Applied Sport Sciences, 9,* 33-41.

Chelladurai, P., Inglis, S.E., and Danylchuk, K.E.(1984). Priorities in intercollegiate athletics: Development of a scale. *Research Quarterly for Exercise and Sport, 55,* 74-79.

Cyert, R.M.,and March, J.G. (1963). *The behavioral theory of the firm.* Englewood Cliffs, N.J.: Prentice-Hall,Inc.

Dessler, G. (1979). *Management fundamentals: A framework.* Reston, Va: Reston Publishing Company.

Eilon, S. (1971). Goals and constraints. *Journal of Management Studies, 8,* 292-303.

Filley, A.C., House, R.J., and Kerr, S. (1976). *Managerial process and organizational behavior.* Glenview,Ill.: Scott, Foreman and Company.

Fink, L.F., Jenks, R.S., and Willits, R.D. (1983). *Designing and managing organizations.* Homewood, Ill.: Richard D. Irwin, Inc.

Gannon, M.J. (1977). *Management: An organizational perspective.* Boston: Little, Brown and Company.

Haggerty, T.R., and Paton, G.A. (1984). *Financial management of sport-related organizations.* Champaign, Ill.: Stipes Publishing Company.

Hall, R.H. (1972). *Organizations: Structure and process.* Englewood Cliffs,N.J.: Prentice-Hall, Inc.

Hasenfeld, Y. (1983). *Human service organizations.* Englewood Cliffs, N.J.: Prentice-Hall, Inc.

Mathews, A.W. (1974). *Athletics in Canadian universities: The report of the AUCC/CIAU study of athletic programs in Canadian universities.* Ottawa: Association of Universities and Colleges of Canada.

McCaskey, M.B. (1974). A contingency approach to planning: Planning with goals and planning without goals. *Academy of Management Journal, 17,* 281-291.

Osborn, A.F. (1953). *Applied imagination.* New York: Charles Scribner's Sons.

Perrow, C. (1961). The analysis of goals in complex organizations. *American Sociological Review, 26,* 854-865.

Radford, K.J. (1975). *Managerial decision making.* Reston, Va.: Reston Publishing Company,Inc.

Richards, M.D. (1978). *Organizational goal structures.* St.Paul,Minn.: West Publishing Company.

Robbins, S.P. (1976). *The administrative process: Integrating theory and practice.* Englewood Cliffs, N.J.: Prentice-Hall,Inc.

Simon, H.A. (1976).*Administrative behavior.* New York: The Free Press.

Soelberg, P. (1967). Unprogrammed decision making. *Industrial Management Review, 8,* 19-29.

Steiner, G.A. (1969). *Top management planning.* New York: Macmillan.

Tannenbaum, R. (1950). Managerial decision making. *Journal of Business, 23,* 22-39.

Thueson, N. (1985). Forecasting the future of sport psychology using the delphi technique.*Psychology of motor behavior and sport: 1985.* Gulf Park, Mississipi, May 1985.

Van de Ven, A.H., and Delbecq, A. (1974). The effectiveness of nominal, delphi, and interacting group decision-making processes. *Academy of Management Journal, 17,* 605-621.

Warriner, C.K. (1965). The problem of organizational purpose. *The Sociological Quarterly, 6,* 139-146.

CHAPTER 4

ORGANIZING

CLASSICAL PRINCIPLES
Specialization
Span of Control
Departmentation
Unity of Command
Responsibility and Authority

BUREAUCRACY
Division of Labor
Hierarchical Authority Structure
A System of Abstract Rules
Impersonality
Technical Competence

CRITICISMS OF BUREAUCRACY

BUREAUCRACY IN A DEMOCRACY

BUREAUCRACY IN SPORT ORGANIZATIONS

ORGANIZING: OPEN SYSTEMS PERSPECTIVES
The Lawrence and Lorsch Model
The Thompson Model
The Parsonian Model

TECHNICAL CORE IN SERVICE ORGANIZATIONS

STRUCTURE OF AUTHORITY IN SERVICE ORGANIZATIONS

SUMMARY

QUESTIONS FOR DISCUSSION

REFERENCES

Once the goals have been specified and the courses of action to achieve those goals have been selected (i.e., after the planning process has been completed), it is necessary to divide the total work into specific jobs, assign these jobs to individuals, and coordinate the activities of these individuals toward the achievement of the organizational goals. This is the process of organizing which, in short, may be defined as "the arrangement of people and tasks to accomplish the goals of the organization" (Fink, Jenks, & Willits, 1983, p. 46). This process results in an organizational structure or design that specifies the relationships among tasks, and among people who perform them.

Filley, House, and Kerr (1976), commenting on the setting up of an organization, noted:

> several ends are sought. First, the structure is designed to provide a means by which many diverse tasks can be systematically allocated. Second, it is expected to provide a system for coordinating the efforts of all toward a common goal. Third, since no real coordination is possible without cooperation, organizational arrangements must be designed to foster rather than hinder cooperation. Fourth, since there can be no coordination or cooperation without communication, the aim is to set up a structure in which there are both recognized formal channels of communication between the incumbents of the various positions, and informal exchange of information to meet the needs of unplanned events. Finally, the structure is designed to allocate decision-making powers in such a way that the decisions will be made by the persons most qualified to make them and have the best available information. (p. 268-269)

In the following sections, the various approaches to achieve the ends suggested by Filley et al. are discussed.

Classical Principles

In the first chapter, reference was made to the classical school of management. In the present section, some of the principles enunciated by the classical theorists regarding the organizing process are outlined. These principles, which have been called "cornerstones of organizing" (Robbins, 1976), include *specialization, span of control, departmentation, unity of command,* and *responsibility and authority.*

Specialization

Specialization refers to the notion that individuals in an organization perform tasks that are narrow in scope. Specialization calls for each person to perform, as far as possible, one function. For an extreme example, consider the assembly line in any factory where one individual's task may be reduced to merely fixing a bolt on the product.

Specialization may be a necessity since one person may not have the time and energy to carry out a number of tasks associated with an organization, or the knowledge to carry out all of them. Also, specialization allows for those with the knowledge and ability to perform skilled tasks, and those without the competency to perform the unskilled tasks.

Specialization, according to Robbins (1976), contributes to efficiency in three specific ways. First, specialization in a limited number of tasks increases the skill or ability to perform those functions. Second, specialization results in the elimination of time spent in putting away tools and equipment from one step and the preparation for another. The third advantage lies in the training of workers. It is easier and more effective to train individuals in a restricted number of specific and routinized tasks.

Span of Control

Span of control is concerned with "how many people, workers, units etc., it is possible for any one supervisor or manager to control effectively and efficiently at any one time" (Fink et al., 1983, p. 53). All of the research conducted in the organizing area generally supports the suggestion that the span of control should be narrow at the top level of management (a ratio of approximately four subordinates to one manager), and wide at the lower levels (a ratio of approximately eight or more subordinates to one manager). A number of references cite research which suggests that seven is the optimum number of subordinates a manager should supervise. However, Fink et al.(1983) have outlined a series of factors that will affect the actual span of control in an organization or unit. These include the type of work done, the competence of the employee, the competence of the supervisor, the relationship between the employee and supervisor, and the pressure for production.

Type of work done. If the employees are engaged in similar and routine tasks, then it is possible for one manager to supervise a large number. If, however, the tasks of the employees are complex and changing, then a narrower span of control is necessary.

Competence and expertise of the person doing the job. If employees are well trained and dedicated to their respective jobs, then close supervision is not necessary. Therefore, the span of control can be wider. On the other hand, individuals with less training need more of a supervisor's time for guidance and direction. Therefore, there should be fewer individuals assigned to a supervisor. Similarly, greater supervision and, therefore, a narrower span of control are required where the workers are indifferent to the task.

Competence/expertise of the supervisor. A more competent and technically qualified supervisor is able to supervise a greater number of subordinates than a less qualified and less skilled supervisor.

Relationship between the supervisor and employees. In situations where there is respect for the supervisor and for the legitimacy of the supervisor's role, and a warm interpersonal relationship is present between supervisor and employees, a wider span of control is feasible.

Pressure for production. If there is pressure on the organization to produce more or better quality goods or services, then the organization must impose greater control and supervision over its employees, which in turn, leads to a narrower span of control.

It should be pointed out that a narrower span of control implies greater control and more supervision while a wider span entails less supervision and less control. Therefore, whenever it is deemed necessary to exert greater control over the subordinates and their tasks, the number of subordinates under a manager is reduced.

When an organization institutes a narrow span of control in its mode of operation, the result is a greater number of levels in the hierarchy. On the other hand, if an organization adopts a wider span of control, the result is fewer levels in the hierarchy. The former situation results in a "tall" structure, while the latter, a "flat" structure.

Departmentation

The principle of span of control leads to the concept of departmentation. That is, "since no one person can administer an unlimited number of subordinates, it is necessary to group activities into some homogeneous formation" (Robbins, 1976, p. 222). This process of forming homogeneous groupings is called departmentation. Filley et al. (1976) distinguished between two broad types of departmentation.

Process-oriented or functional departmentation is based on the concept of specialization. That is, individuals performing the same functions are grouped together under one department. A sales department, and an accounting department in a business firm, and a physical education department in a high school are examples of departmentation according to specialized functions.

Another way of grouping is called *goal-oriented departmentation* which "is usually based on division of the organization according to different products, different geographical areas, different customer types, or different projects" (Filley et al., 1976, p. 361). In this type of departmentation, each unit consists of members with different specialized skills performing different functions. Consider a profit-oriented fitness club which has expanded its business to different geographical areas. Each geographical unit must hire people of different skills to perform the necessary functions. Similarly, when the firm decides to cater to two different sets of customers, namely, those who seek general conditioning and those who prepare for athletic competitions, it may be necessary to create two departments each utilizing the services of personnel of different skills.

A number of advantages and disadvantages are associated with the two forms of departmentation. According to Filley et al. (1976), functional departmentation provides for the development of sub-specialities (a division of labor within a speciality); advancement in the speciality; supervision by a specialist; professional contagion (i.e., the opportunity to learn from professional colleagues and to be motivated by them); maximum use of resources (i.e., existing personnel or equipment is utilized to the maximum extent before additions are made); and satisfaction with work (i.e., members of functional departments are more satisfied with their work than members of goal-oriented departments).

On the negative side, functional departmentation leads to difficulties in coordinating and scheduling the activities of different units. Also, functional structures lead to conflict and competition between departments due to differences in professional orientations of the personnel of the departments concerned. That is, "the goals of the profession or speciality rather than the goals of the customer or project are emphasized" (Filley et al., 1976, p. 365).

The advantages of goal-oriented departmentation are that the units

> *tend to focus attention on customer, environmental, or project requirements. That is, the energies of the people and the evaluation of their programs depend more upon the solution of the problem or the accomplishment of organizational goals than the day-to-day routines of a functional structure. (Filley et al., 1976, p. 367)*

Since, in such departmentation, personnel of different specialized skills function under one manager, there is greater coordination and less conflict among members. However, goal-oriented departmentation is less efficient in the sense that skills and/or equipment are duplicated and they are not fully utilized. Further, since supervision by a specialist is denied to most of the members, they may feel isolated — particularly if there are no others in the same speciality. That is, the opportunities for learning and professional growth are minimized.

Matrix structure is another form of departmentation which attempts to capitalize on the advantages of both the functional and goal-oriented modes of departmentation. A matrix organization is simply the imposition of one structure over the other. In Exhibit 4.1, members of a faculty of physical education belonging to a particular subject area are grouped together as a functional unit. At the same time, each individual member belongs to a goal-oriented unit. This allows for greater and more efficient coordination in a project's activities while, at the same time, providing a "home base" for each member. However, there is one serious drawback in the matrix structure. Each member is supervised by two different managers which is a violation of the principle of *unity of command* which is discussed below.

Exhibit 4.1. Matrix Structure of a Faculty of Physical Education.

FUNCTIONAL GROUPING (SUBJECT AREAS)	PROJECT GROUPING (PROGRAMS)			
	UNDERGRADUATE	GRADUATE	ATHLETICS	INTRAMURALS
SOCIAL SCIENCE				
BIO-SCIENCE				
ACTIVITY SCIENCE				

Unity of Command

Unity of command is similar to the Biblical principle "No one can serve two masters." It means that "...each person should take orders from and be accountable to only one supervisor" (Filley et al., 1976, p. 269). This serves to protect against the possibility that conflicting commands will be given by different superiors. While the unity of command concept is useful in highly structured organizations such as a government bureaucracy, it is likely to be disregarded in more modern, complex forms of organizational structure like the matrix organization. In such structures, an employee may be expected to follow the advice and suggestions of more than one person rather than to strictly comply with the directives of one supervisor.

Responsibility and Authority

The principle of responsibility with equal authority states that an employee must be given the necessary authority required to carry out an assigned responsibility. It is readily apparent that individuals cannot carry out their duties if they do not have the authority to make decisions relating to their tasks. Thus, a physical education teacher must have the authority to decide on the content and process of a class if he/she is to carry out the teaching responsibilities. This notion of authority equalling responsibility becomes critical in the case of those who have to monitor and control the activities of the subordinates.

In summary, the principles of specialization, span of control, departmentation, unity of command, and responsibility and authority are intended to enable the organization to function efficiently and without friction. Almost all organizations embrace these principles to varying degrees.

Bureaucracy

Bureaucrats have been likened to cockroaches. Like cockroaches, they are everywhere; like cockroaches, they don't seem to serve any useful purpose; and like cockroaches, they seem to defy all attempts at their extinction (from Paperland, Film Board of Canada).

This description sums up the negative attitude of anybody who has come into contact with a bureaucracy. But, despite all criticisms, bureaucratic organizations are dominant in all nations, whether they are democratic or totalitarian, rich or poor, large or small. As Perrow (1972) pointed out, a bureaucracy is

a form of organization superior to all others we know or can hope to afford in the near and middle future; the chances of doing away with it or changing it are probably nonexistent in the West in this century. Thus it is crucial to understand it and appreciate it (p. 7).

Although bureaucracy has been practiced in some form or another in ancient times, the analyses and discussion of the phenomenon has only gained momentum from the beginning of this century. Classical theorists like Taylor and Fayol had also emphasized some of the characteristics of a bureaucratic organization. But it was left to Max Weber, a German sociologist, to coin the term "bureaucracy" and write extensively on the concept in the early part of the century. In his writings, Weber (1947) emphasized that an organization, if it is to operate rationally and efficiently, must be structured to include certain fundamental characteristics. His bureaucratic tenets (or principles) are discussed below. It must be noted that some of these tenets are the same or similar to the classical principles of organizations detailed earlier.

Division of Labor

In any organization, the total work must be broken down into simple, well-defined tasks, and these tasks must be distributed to members as official duties. As noted previously, division of labor encourages specialization which in turn leads to greater productivity and efficiency in recruitment and training of members. Weber also emphasized that since the division of labor defines the responsibility of individual members, there is greater control over the organizational activities.

Hierarchical Authority Structure

The positions in the organization are arranged in a hierarchical manner so that progressively increasing authority is vested at each successively higher level. That is, each level in the hierarchy has the right to issue orders to the level below, and the duty to obey orders from the level above.

Weber (1958) emphasized that authority in a bureaucracy resides in a *position* in the organization and not in the *person* who occupies it. Such authority emanates from and is governed by written rules and regulations. This was referred to by Weber as *rational-legal authority* since the investment and distribution of authority among the different positions in the organization is rational and legally binding within the organization. He contrasted rational-legal authority with both *traditional authority* and *charismatic authority*.

Traditional authority is based on custom and precedents. That is, there is a common understanding that a particular individual will exercise a given level of authority because it has always been the case. Such authority "is anchored in an established belief in the sanctity of the status of those exercising authority in the past" (Hoy and Miskel, 1982, p. 79). Thus, young athletes might obey the unreasonable demands of a highly autocratic coach because all the athletes in previous years had done so.

Charismatic authority is a function of the followers' belief in the leader's special gifts or espoused mission. The authority of charisma, as Hoy and Miskel (1983) noted:

> results primarily from the leader's overwhelming personal appeal, and typically a common value orientation emerges within the group to produce an intense normative commitment to identification with the person. (p. 79)

It is quite conceivable that the young athletes referred to above might exhibit obedience to whatever their coach said because of the coach's charismatic authority. Although individuals in an organization may experience all three types of authority, Weber insisted that only the compliance based on the rational-legal authority contributes to the efficiency of the organization.

A hierarchical authority structure ensures that there is control of activities at every level of the organization. It also serves to establish a clear channel of communication within the organization (i.e., who communicates official messages to whom). A fact that is very often overlooked is that the same hierarchy which vests authority in a position also sets the boundaries within which such authority can be exercised.

A System of Abstract Rules

Another principle of a bureaucracy outlined by Weber is a system of abstract rules. This principle makes reference to the fact that an organization will specify a set of rules which "define what is to be done, by whom, and for whom under what conditions" (Sofer, 1972, p. 9). Individuals and/or incidents are systematically classified into categories and a set of rules is specified for each and every category. The employee is expected to apply the rules relevant to a particular situation. For example, the locker room attendant follows a set of rules for determining who is eligible for a locker and/or gym apparel. The clients in the locker room belong to one of the categories of faculty member, student or team member; and the rules specify a particular set of services for each category.

The system of abstract rules ensures that there is consistency and uniformity in the activities of the organization and its members. That is, for any given situation, the treatment provided is the same, irrespective of the members involved or the time and place in which the situation arises.

Impersonality

According to Weber, bureaucracies also exhibit impersonality. Impersonality refers to the notion that employees of an organization must deal with clients/customers and/or subordinates/superiors on the same categorical basis without any personal, emotional, or social considerations. That is, a "social distance" must be maintained in dealing with the affairs of the organization. The locker room attendant in the above example cannot be influenced by personal likes and dislikes for a client. This tenet is also aimed at uniformity and consistency in the organizational activities.

Technical Competence

In a bureaucracy, employees are hired and promoted only on the basis of their competence relevant to a particular office/position in the organization. Technical competence supplements the notion of rational-legal authority discussed earlier. The authority of a position cannot be considered to be rational if the occupants of that position do not possess the requisite competence. Thus, when a basketball coach does not have expertise in the technical aspects of the game as well as knowledge of the psychological and physiological aspects of training and competition, the players cannot be expected to accept his/her authority as rational and binding.

In summary, Weber argued that the organizations which possess division of labor, a hierarchical authority structure, a system of abstract rules, impersonality, and technical competence are rational and efficient (that is, all activities are aimed at achieving the organizational goals efficiently). It has been pointed out by some authors that some of the tenets of bureaucracy occur naturally — belong to the natural order. For example, even the human body is characterized by a division of labor (different systems of the body carry out different functions), and a hierarchy (the brain controlling the rest of the body). Thus, when an organization is created or develops, some of the tenets of a bureaucracy must naturally follow.

Criticisms of Bureaucracy

It is worth noting that Weber was describing an "ideal" construct. As is most often the case, the ideal is never reached. The result has been that there are some serious criticisms levelled against a bureaucracy and its prescriptions.

The major criticism against the creation of a *division of labor* is that each individual's job is reduced to a monotonous and degrading routine. The reduced content of the job leads, in turn, to decreased initiative, creativity, and motivation. The resultant boredom and frustration have been known to reduce productivity of the workers. Thus, a division of labor which could produce expertise and, through it, efficiency, could also lead to boredom and inefficiency.

Deparmentation, which is division of labor at the unit level, creates inter-departmental rivalry which, in turn, leads to the displacement of organizational goals. That is, each department sets and pursues its own goals without reference to the wider organizational goals.

A serious drawback to *hierarchy of authority* is that the communication flow ultimately becomes inconsistent with the work flow. Two employees handling the case of a client may belong to two different authority units. Although they may be closely connected to the case, and work in close proximity to each other, they cannot communicate with each other and make decisions officially. Each must communicate through a different superior. This indirect form of communication leads to delays in the work process.

The tenet of *abstract rules* has drawn the severest criticisms. First, quite often the rules become outdated and out of tune with modern conditions.For instance, until recently, the immigration laws of Canada stated that a foreign female who married a Canadian became a Canadian citizen automatically. But a foreign male who married a Canadian was required to go through the regular procedures to become a citizen. Presumably, this law was established when social conditions and societal expectations concerning the roles of females and males were different. Times changed but the law remained the same.

A second issue concerns the application of appropriate rules. That is, a bureaucrat must first place the incident or subject into the proper category. But, errors in categorization may result in inappropriate treatment in some cases.

Third, the existence of rules, in effect, sets the minimum acceptable level of performance for employees. The rules reduce the initiative of the workers who then tend to strictly conform to the rules. The result is that rules which were only intended to serve as a means to an end are treated as ends in themselves. Finally, reliance on rules makes employees rigid in their interactions with clients. This rigidity produces tension between employee and clients which, in turn, leads the employees to adhere even more closely to the rules. This phenomenon is reflected in the common phrase "throwing the book at you".

The notion of *impersonality* overlooks the community of humans inside and outside the organization. Critics of the impersonality of a bureaucracy have argued that it is not realistic to expect employees to suppress all their interpersonal feelings and attitudes.

Technical competence is generally accepted as a requisite for organizational efficiency and effectiveness. However, bureaucracies tend to promote individuals to higher positions on the basis of seniority. Although seniority often reflects experience and accrued knowledge at various lower level positions, promotion on the basis of seniority denies the gifted and the bright the opportunity to move up the hierarchy. And, it could be argued that in some bureaucracies"twenty years' experience is one year's experience twenty times over".

Despite these criticisms, many organization theorists supported the ideas of Weber and endorsed the view that the bureaucracy should be the dominant mode of structuring large and complex organizations. Perrow (1972) has gone even further when he suggested that "the sins generally attributed to bureaucracy are either not sins at all or are consequences of the failure to bureaucratize sufficiently" (p. 6). But, Perrow also acknowledged that the 'ideal' form of a bureaucracy is never realized. One of the reasons for this is that members of the organization "track all kinds of mud from the rest of their lives with them into the organization, and they have all kinds of interests that are independent of the organization" (p. 5). Another reason is that people "are only indifferently intelligent, prescient, all-knowing, and energetic. All organizations must be designed for the 'average' person one is likely to find in each position, not the superman" (p. 5).

Perrow also pointed out that a bureaucracy is structured to be stable in order to be efficient. In the case of governments, the stability requirement may be the most critical criteria. But, one paradox is that if the stability requirement is achieved, the bureaucracy becomes impervious to changes in the environment. In turn, this results in the development of so-called red tape and inefficiency. Government bureaucracies are often strongly criticized for their stability and the red tape and/or inefficiency which result. However, it is also important to remember that it is the stability of a bureaucracy which provides some form of consistency in periods of rapid and dramatic change (democratic or revolutionary) in the government.

Bureaucracy in a Democracy

It has been argued that the emphasis placed on the establishment of a hierarchy, and the discipline and obedience to superiors which are inherent components of a bureaucracy are antithetical to the democratic notions of equality, freedom of choice, and dissent. If this is the case, how could a bureaucracy be tolerated and allowed to grow in a democracy?

Blau (1956) resolved this issue by outlining the contrasting purposes and processes of a democracy and a bureaucracy. The purpose of a democracy is to identify commonly agreed social objectives. The process of identifying these goals occurs through freedom of expression and dissent. Based on these differing expressions, the electorate and/or lawmakers can then make an informed judgement.

In contrast, the purpose of a bureaucracy is to achieve specified goals. Its concern is with the determination and implementation of efficient ways of achieving those goals. In order to achieve efficiency, rules and procedures must be specified, and an authority structure instituted to ensure adherence to the rules. Also, members must exhibit disciplined compliance to the rules and obedience to authority. Thus, as Blau (1956) pointed out:

> Bureaucratic and democratic structures can be distinguished, then, on the basis of the dominant organizing principle; efficiency or freedom of dissent. Each of these principles is suited for one purpose and not the another. When people set themselves the task of determining the social objectives that represent the interests of most of them, the crucial problem is to provide an opportunity for all conflicting viewpoints to be heard. In contrast, when the task is the achievement of given social objectives the essential problem to be solved is to discover the efficient, not the popular, means for doing so. Democratic values require not only that social goals be determined by majority decision, but also that they be implemented through the most effective methods available, that is, by establishing organizations that are bureaucratically rather than democratically governed. The existence, therefore, of such bureaucracies does not violate democratic values. (p. 107).

The contrasting objectives and processes of a democracy and a bureaucracy are illustrated in Exhibit 4.2.

Exhibit 4.2. Purposes and Processes of a Democracy and a Bureaucracy.

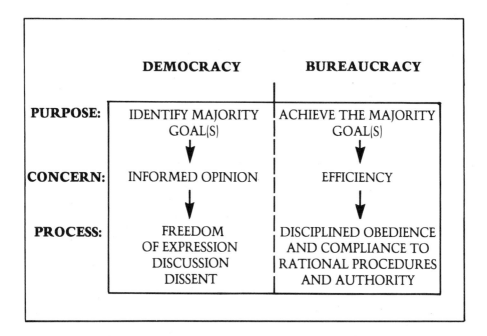

Although theorists like Perrow and Blau have supported the concept of bureaucracy, they have also pointed out the threat posed by large bureaucracies. Because of their control over vast amounts of resources (people and money), large bureaucracies have the power to influence the democratic processes. In fact, their tendency to perpetuate themselves and to increase their power, lead them to interfere in the affairs of the democracy. For instance, the lobbying efforts of government agencies (e.g., the Pentagon in the U.S.A) or large corporations (e.g., AT&T) to influence the decision making processes of democratically elected bodies are just a few examples. Perrow (1972) provided a caution when he noted that

> it is also crucial to understand not only how it [bureaucracy] mobilizes social resources for desirable ends, but also how it inevitably concentrates those forces in the hands of a few who are prone to use them for ends we do not approve of, for ends we are generally not aware of, and more frightening still, for ends we are led to accept because we are not in a position to conceive alternative ones. (p. 7)

In overview, it seems reasonable to suggest that a bureaucracy in a democracy is value neutral — the positive and negative consequences are produced by humans in bureaucracies.

Bureaucracy in Sport Organizations

The concept of bureaucracy has been discussed at length for two main reasons. First, modern society is controlled/dominated to a greater and greater extent by bureaucracies (the government, large corporations, universities, hospitals, unions, political parties, etc.). Thus, all individuals must have an understanding and appreciation of the principles underlying bureaucratic structures. Second, although the concept of a bureaucracy appears to be relevant only to large organizations, the elements that make a bureaucracy rational and efficient can be profitably applied to smaller organizations. For example, in the case of football, the most successful teams are clearly characterized by a division of labor (offensive and defensive units, and the specializations within each), a hierarchy (the chief coach, assistant coach, coaches for specialized units, the captain, quarterback), impersonality in selection, utilization and rewarding of athletes, and technical competence on the part of the coaches and players. Further, rules are numerous in football varying from the rules of the sport to the league rules and to the team rules which even control the athlete's life away from the field. What is most significant is that these rules are closely followed by the players. There is no better example of members' willing compliance and obedience to the rules and authority of a bureaucracy.

Frisby (1983) noted that a number of authors

have bemoaned the loss of personal autonomy on the part of the participants and volunteers, the intrusion of the law and government into the arena of sport, and the usurpation of expressive values by instrumental values as sport has become more bureaucratic in nature. (p. 80)

Their concerns that the fundamental elements of sport are lost with bureaucratization are somewhat analogous to the concerns expressed about bureaucracy in relation to a democracy. In the latter context, Blau (1956), as noted earlier, argued that the contrasting purposes of a democracy and a bureaucracy necessitate as well as justify different processes — freedom of expression and dissent in a democracy, and compliance and obedience in a bureaucracy. Similarly, an examination of the purposes of competitive and recreational sports, reveals that they are radically different, and consequently, the process within each differs. In this regard, Keating (1964) has distinguished between *athletics*, whose purpose is pursuit of excellence, and *sport*, whose purpose is maximizing pleasure for both contestants:

In essence, sport is a kind of diversion which has for its immediate and direct end fun, pleasure and delight and which is dominated by a spirit of moderation and generosity. Athletics on the other hand, is essentially competitive activity which has for its end victory in the contest and which is characterized by a spirit of dedication, sacrifice, and intensity. (p. 28)

If the differences between recreational sport (which is concerned with the pursuit of pleasure) and athletics or competitive sport (which is concerned with the pursuit of excellence) are taken into account, then it is only logical to expect that the two endeavors will be structured differently. Recreational sport must be loosely structured; competitive sport, bureaucratically structured.

The relevance of bureaucratic concepts to national sport organizations is illustrated by Frisby's (1983) study of those organizations in Canada. She found that those national sport organizations that were more bureaucratic were also more effective in terms of both goal attainment and resource acquisition. She contended that "Weber's theory of bureaucracy provides a useful framework for understanding the nature of voluntary amateur sport organizations" (p. 246). Even voluntary organizations must rely on bureaucratic processes if they wish to achieve specific goals.

Organizing: Open Systems Perspectives

A bureaucracy is, by nature, a closed organizational system. In the bureaucratic view, the organizational goals are assumed to be clear and fixed, and the organization and its processes are designed to be efficient in all its internal operations. In its drive for efficiency, a bureaucracy tends to ignore the environmental influences. But organizations do not operate in a vacuum. Fundamentally, an organization is an instrument of society and, consequently, it has a primary responsibility to society and its needs. Because societal needs change, it is essential for any organization to monitor the changes and adapt in function in order to more effectively meet the needs of society. Even if it is accepted that organizations are self serving, they must still adapt and change with the changes in the environment in order to survive. Since an organization is dependent upon the environment for its resources as well as the disposal of its outputs, it becomes imperative that an organization must be attuned to the vagaries of the environment. Thus, a technical college must recruit students and, in turn, those students must eventually find a place in the work force. But, if the technological needs of society change and the technical college does not modify its curriculum to reflect these changes, it could be eventually forced out of business. This sensitivity to the demands of the environment forms the basis for the approach taken by many of the modern theorists in the designing of organizations. In the following sections, the approaches taken by three of those theorists —Lawrence and Lorsch (1967), Thompson (1967), and Parsons (1960) — are discussed.

The Lawrence and Lorsch Model

The research of Lawrence and Lorsch (1967) was concerned with manufacturing organizations. Their basic premise was that a manufacturing organization is basically divided into three major subsystems: sales, production, and research and development. Each of these subsystems must deal with different segments of the environment — market, technical-economic, and scientific sub-environments respectively.

The three subsystems differ with respect to the rate at which their respective sub-environments change, in the relative amounts of information they have about their environments, and in the feedback they receive from the environment. These three elements constitute what Lawrence and Lorsch called "certainty of the environment".According to these authors, the relative certainty of the environment faced by the subsystems creates two specific problems for the organization — *differentiation* and *integration*.

Differentiation. Differentiation occurs when an organization is divided into units according to environmental exigencies, and those units are then staffed with people of appropriate attitude and skills. It must be noted that the concept of differentiation is not identical to the concept of departmentation. According to the classical and bureaucratic approaches, departmentation occurs when an organization is divided into units that are concerned with specific functions and/or purposes. The internal structure within the various units is similar and is characterized by hierarchy of authority and rules and regulations.

But differentiation, according to Lawrence and Lorsch, is division of labor based on the differing environmental conditions. And, since each unit is required to interact with different segments of the environment (and these segments differ in terms of uncertainty and rate of change), each organizational unit must be organized differently to enable it to cope up with the particular environment and its requirements. Further, a necessary condition for differentiation is that the members of a unit possess those specific talents and attitudes that are consistent with the demands of the environment.

Integration. Lawrence and Lorsch pointed out that while differentiation is relatively easy to implement, integrating the subunits into a meaningful and effective whole is a problem. Because differentiated units have different structures and follow different operating procedures, (and, more importantly, the members of these units have different training and orientations), the task of integration is more difficult than the task of differentiation. It is possible for organizations to achieve the difficult task of integration by creating liaison or integrator roles, by making interactions across groupings mandatory, by promoting joint responsibilities for common goals, by developing task forces or committees with joint memberships, and/or by holding meetings to foster familiarity among areas.

Although the Lawrence and Lorsch model was developed for business firms and industries, the concepts of differentiation and integration are also useful in the context of sport organizations. This is certainly the case for the organization of the programs of undergraduate physical education, graduate physical education, intercollegiate athletics and intramurals within a university context. The "classical" organization structures illustrated in Exhibit 4.3 are characteristic of many physical education departments.

Coaches, administrators, and other faculty members working within the classical structures presented in Exhibit 4.3 are familiar with the longstanding discussions, arguments, and debates which revolve around questions of control, jurisdiction, and responsibility. These discussions become particularly heated when intercollegiate athletic programs deviate (or are perceived to deviate) from the fundamental educational mandate of the university. Unfortunately, however, these discussions do not address fundamental organizational issues relating to the goals of each program, the environments

Exhibit 4.3. Some Structural Configurations of Physical Education, Athletics, and Intramurals in a University.

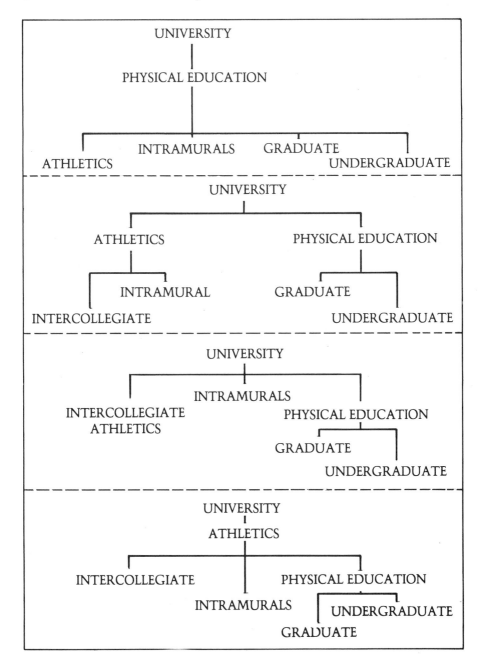

they have to deal with, or the required internal structures and processes within each program.

If the concept of differentiation is applied to a department of physical education, the four programs might be organized according to the structure illustrated in Exhibit 4.4.

*Exhibit 4.4.*Differentiation and Integration of Physical Education, Athletics, and Intramural, from an Open Systems Perspective.
Adapted from Behling & Schrisheim (1976).

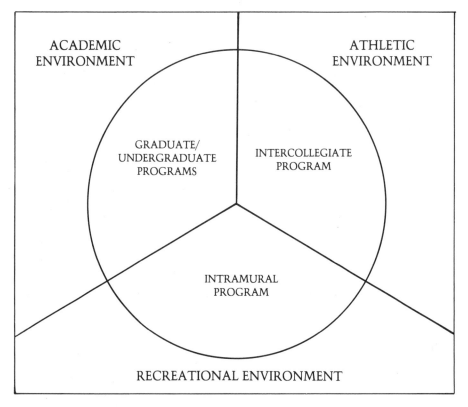

Since each of the four programs has different sets of goals, and since they interact with different environments, they would be allowed to adopt those structures and processes appropriate to their situation (differentiation). For example, the purpose of the undergraduate program is to provide a general education to a large number of students, and that education must be comparable to that offered within other faculties. Thus, the undergraduate program must be more structured than the graduate program. Further, teaching receives greater emphasis in the undergraduate program while research is emphasized to a greater degree in the graduate program. Thus, the undergraduate program must be relatively more bureaucratized than the graduate program — there must be a greater concern with consistency and uniformity of operations.

The concept of differentiation also requires that those members involved in the undergraduate and graduate programs have different talents and skills. Faculty in the undergraduate program must have the talents to teach a large number of students and to follow a prespecified curriculum (which implies that the course is offered within a stable environment). On the other hand, graduate professors must be oriented more toward research, possess the capacity to handle the few elite students who seek their advice, and have the ability to generate and solve novel problems.

Even the undergraduate programs of different universities can be organized differently according to whether their programs are oriented toward professional preparation or toward general education. Chelladurai (1976), adapting a model proposed by Bell (1974), presented two differentiated models of physical education programs — the factory model and the service model. These are contrasted in Exhibit 4.5.

Exhibit 4.5. Factory and Service Models of Physical Education Programs.

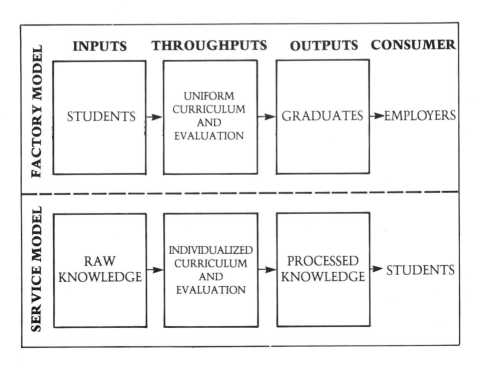

In the *factory* model, students are considered as inputs who are converted into outputs (graduates with specific competencies). The consumers of these outputs are the future employers of these graduates and society in general. Thus, the employers' needs and requirements are paramount in the determination of the required competencies and skills. With the factory model, there must be standardization of the procedures relating to the recruitment of students, the design of curriculum, the mode of instruction and evaluation, and the recruitment and evaluation of faculty members.

In the *service* model, the students are considered the ultimate consumers of the knowledge processed by the faculty members. Accordingly, the students' desires and preferences have greater influence in the types of courses offered. There is also less emphasis on the uniformity of the skills and competencies of the students in the service model. Therefore, there is also less standardization in the procedures relating to student recruitment, curriculum development, instruction and evaluation, faculty competencies, and their evaluation.

The internal structures as well as the skills, orientations, and attitudes of both the students and faculty would be different in the two models presented in Exhibit 4.5. Moreover, the two models would serve different purposes and be effective in two different environments. This is, in fact, the essence of the concept of differentiation.

While the undergraduate, graduate, intramural, and athletic programs are easily segregated, integrating them into a meaningful whole in the pursuit of the larger organizational goals requires careful thought and conscious effort. This notion of integration is achieved differently in different universities. One obvious method is to place one of these programs in a superior position to the other programs, and assign it the responsibility and the authority to coordinate the activities of all programs. Historically, universities have followed one of the patterns illustrated in Exhibit 4.3. But, more recently, the overall responsibility has been delegated to the academic programs. That is, physical education has been charged with the control of the intercollegiate and intramural programs. Typically, the dean or chairperson of physical education has been given the responsibility of supervising all the four programs. In some instances, an attempt has been made to achieve the required integration through policy statements and rules and procedures, but, these have only been partially successful. More effective integration has been achieved when the managers of the four programs have been brought together in face-to-face encounters to confront each other over any contentious issues. This is achieved by formally bringing the four unit heads together in the form of a committee which meets periodically. This process of direct confrontation has been recommended by Lawrence and Lorsch as an effective integrative mechanism.

Another factor which can contribute to the integration of the four programs is the employment of individuals who have responsibilities spread across two or more programs. Thus, a professor might teach an undergraduate course and also coach a university team. In this situation, faculty members are expected to develop an understanding of the requirements, constraints, and values of the two programs, and, therefore, to integrate their activities across both.

The Thompson Model

Thompson (1967) also endorsed the Lawrence and Lorsch view that an organization should be subdivided into units on the basis of the segments of the environment with which they interact. Those units that have direct contact with the external environment are called the *boundary spanning units*. In addition, Thompson, following Parsons(1960), endorsed the view that organizations must attempt to seal off one of the units — the *technical core* —from the environmental uncertainties.

Technical core refers to the unit that is most directly concerned with the production of goods or services. The assembly line in an automobile factory, the classrooms in a high school, or an athletic team in an intercollegiate athletic program are examples of the technical core in their respective organizations. Thompson argued that if the technical core is to be efficient, it must be able to work in a stable environment in terms of steady flow of inputs, prompt disposal of its outputs, and minimal interference from other organizations. That is, the technical core must be able to focus on its fundamental task of producing goods or services without being distracted by environmental concerns such as securing inputs and disposing of outputs.

This environmental stability is provided by what Thompson called the *boundary spanning units*. As Thompson (1967) pointed out:

> *organizations subject to rationality norms seek to isolate their technical cores from environmental influences by establishing boundary-spanning units to buffer or level environmental fluctuations. These responsibilities help determine the structure of input and output units. (p. 67)*

In business and industry, units like marketing, purchasing, legal, and public relations interact with their respective task environments in their unique ways, and secure the resources needed for the technical core, dispose of its outputs and, thus, create a relatively stable environment for the technical core.

The relevance of the Thompson model to sport organizations can be highlighted through one or two examples. The teacher and students in a course constitute the technical core of the university. The classroom is where the fundamental function of a university (i.e., teaching) is carried out. For the teacher and the students to carry on their respective tasks — teaching and learning — they must be protected from disturbances which could arise from outside the immediate classroom situation. The buffer between the technical core and outer environment is composed of the dean, program chairpersons, and other administrative officers within the faculty, members of the registrar's office, employees in the physical plant, reservation office, and time-tabling office, the president, and other members of the upper management of the university. Exhibit 4.6 illustrates the insulation of the classroom by the administrative units of the university.

Exhibit 4.6. Thompson's Model Applied to a Faculty of Physical Education.
Adapted from Behling & Schriesheim (1976).

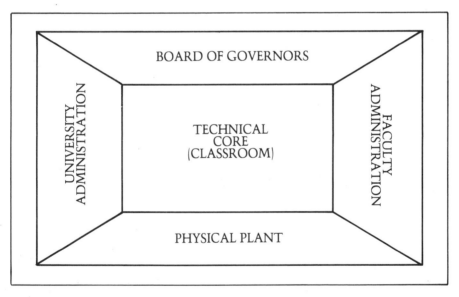

Typically, these buffer agents handle the admission of the students to the university, the general program of studies, entrance requirements into the particular course, the scheduling of classes and exams, reservation of classrooms and so on. The major concerns of the teacher are to teach the course according to the prepared course outline and to evaluate the students. The students, after they have selected the course, are concerned only with learning. Scholarships, bursaries, and student loans are also a buffering mechanism in the sense that they permit students to concentrate on their studies rather than spend time trying to earn money for upkeep. On a wider scale, the top officials of the university interact with the environmental groups such as government or private corporations in order to secure the necessary resources for the university. One of their main functions is to smooth out fluctuations imposed by the disturbances in the distal environment.

The operation of a university athletic team also illustrates the notion of protecting the technical core from environmental disturbances. Because the athletic team must strive for excellence in the sport and attempt to win as many games as possible, its major focus must be on training and preparation. All factors and influences that might deter from this exclusive focus must be blocked out. Athletic departments do this, in part, by providing athletic scholarships in order to relieve the athlete of the concerns for his/her upkeep. Some universities also have separate dormitories for athletes in order to filter out the "distracting influences" of other students. And, finally in some universities, special classes and/or instructors are provided so that activities scheduled (practices and games) are not affected by regularly scheduled classes. While many educators question such practices in a university setting, it cannot be denied that those institutions which adapt these strategies —provide a buffer between the technical core and the outer environment —nurture, develop, and produce the best athletic talent.[1]

The Parsonian Model

Parsons' (1960) model is particularly relevant to those sport organizations which have both an elected and appointed body of administrators (i.e., the organization has both volunteer administrators and paid professional administrators).

In Parsons' view an organization consists of three distinct hierarchical suborganizations — the *technical,* the *managerial,* and the *institutional* subsystems. These are illustrated in Exhibit 4.7.

The *technical subsystem* is concerned with those activities that are directly associated with the major task(s) of the organization. The nature of the technical task and the processes involved define its fundamental requirements. This is identical to Thompson's conceptualization.

The *managerial subsystem* is a higher order system which both administers and serves the technical system. Parsons (1960) attributed two major areas of responsibility to the managerial subsystem:

1. This concept of insulating the athletes from environmental influences is also evident in the manner in which the communist bloc countries prepare their athletes. Typically, good athletes are recruited and employed by a factory or a government agency like the army, etc. Their salary is equivalent to the athletic scholarships received at a North American university. Instead of reporting for regular work, the athletes report for athletic practices. The work requirements are rescheduled to fit the athletic schedule just as is the case in some North American universities. Thus, in both cases, Thompson's idea of protecting the technical core is largely followed.

Exhibit 4.7. Parsons' Hierchical Differentiaiton of System Activities.
Adapted from Behling & Schriesheim (1976).

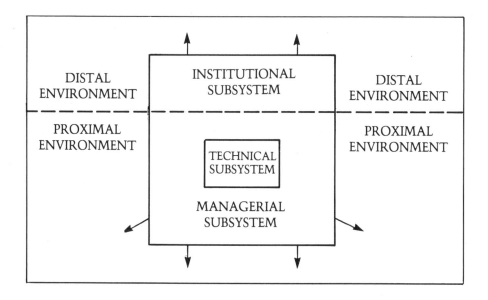

The primary one is to mediate between the technical organization and those who use its "products"—the "customers", pupils or whoever. The second is to procure the resources necessary for carrying out the technical functions (i.e., financial resources, personnel and physical facilities). (p. 62)

Thus, the managerial subsystem carries out part of the boundary spanning functions included in Thompson's model.

Finally, the function of the *institutional system* is to interact with the wider environment with which the organization must deal. As Parsons (1960) noted:

the organization which consists of both technical and managerial suborganizations never operates subject only to the exigencies of disposal to and procurement from other agencies (which stand on an approximately equal level) as customers or as sources of supply. There is always some "organized superior" agency with which the organization articulates. (p. 63)

This interaction with the wider social system serves to legitimize the existence of the focal organization and justify the societal support extended to it.

From Parsons' perspective, the institutional system in a typical organization consists of the Board of Governors or Directors. Their functions are mainly to set the objectives and policies of the organization, to recruit the top managers, and more importantly, to direct the institutional system's efforts toward the management of that segment of the environment for which it is responsible. Thus, after charting the major course for the organization, the institutional system must deal with the larger environment with a view to securing necessary resources. It must also work to legitimize the organization in the eyes of the public.

The significance of the institutional system and its function is best illustrated by the recent history of the Chrysler Corporation. When that corporation had some serious financial difficulties, the institutional system was able to approach the government and banks and secure the loans necessary to keep the company viable. The arguments advanced in favor of such assistance were mainly related to the company's contribution to the overall welfare of society. In short, an organization must be able to justify its existence to the larger society and to secure its support.

There are numerous similarities between Thompson's model and Parsons's model.[2] This is not surprising since Thompson's model is partly derived from Parsons'. In both models, the need to seal off the technical core from environmental influences, and to create boundary spanning units is acknowledged. But, there is a difference in how the two models distribute the boundary spanning activities to the various subsystems. In Thompson's model, various departments are expected to deal with various segments of the environment. For example, the purchasing department interacts with suppliers, while the sales department interacts with customers. In contrast, in Parsons' model, the total environment is subdivided into proximal (or task) and distal environments (see Chapter Two). Parsons proposed that the responsibilities for these two segments of the environment must be split by hierarchical levels. That is, while the managerial subsystem must deal with the immediate task environment (including customers and suppliers), the institutional subsystem must interact with the larger segment of the environment, (the society at large). In the example of the Chrysler corporation referred to earlier, the institutional subsystem interacted with the government and banks while the managerial subsystem dealt with the elements in

2. Recently, Mintzberg (1979) proposed a model consisting of five subsystems — the strategic apex, the middle line, the operating core, the technostructure, and the support staff. The Mintzberg model can be conceived of as a refinement and synthesis of the models of Parsons and Thompson. That is, Parsons' hierarchical differentiation is maintained by Mintzberg in the form of strategic apex, the middle line managers, and the operating core. Also, the horizontal differentiation proposed by Thompson is evident in Mintzberg's model since he designated the technostructure (consisting of analysts and their staff) and support staff as auxilary units — they perform essential functions but are not directly linked to the operating core.

the immediate task environment such as the suppliers and labor unions.

Parsons further argued that although the hierarchy places the institutional system above the managerial system which, in turn, is above the technical system, there must be a clear break in the simple continuity of the authority structure. The two interfaces (i.e., between the institutional and managerial subsystems, and between the managerial and technical subsystems) must be designed in such a way that one system does not interfere with the functioning of the other two subsystems. That is, "the institutionalization of these relations must typically take a form where the relative independence of each is protected" (Parsons, 1960, p. 69).

The idea of insulating the technical core in a university was discussed in the earlier section concerned with Thompson's model for an organization. Parsons' concept of differentiation along hierarchical levels also is very meaningful in the context of sport organizations. For example, in the case of physical education classes in schools, the relevant institutional subsystem is the Board of Education. It consists, of course, of members elected from the public. The board sets the broad policies and guidelines for the school system and hires the top executives. In turn, the top executives are given the authority to execute the Board's policies. A major responsibility of the Board (the institutional system in this example) is to interact with the government and other agencies which control the resources necessary for the operation of the overall school system.

The managerial subsystem in this example consists of the executive officers and the principals of the individual schools. Their responsibilities lie in the areas of admission of students, hiring of qualified teachers, procurement of supplies and equipment, scheduling of classes, and so on. All of these activities are aimed at stabilizing and smoothing the conditions for the technical core — the teachers and students in every classroom.

Parsons' ideas are also very relevant to those organizations which govern the various sports at the national or state level. As is the case with local school systems, a Board of Governors (or Directors) is elected and charged with the promotion and development of a sport. It represents the institutional system for the organization. The managerial subsystem may consist of an executive committee or paid professional administrators, or both. In the case of elite sport, the national team, which consists of the athletes, the coach, and the assistants, represents the technical core. Since the coach has been hired or appointed (put in charge of the technical core — the team) on the basis of expertise, the entire operation of the team should be left to his/her discretion. This includes the recruitment and selection of athletes, their training, the scheduling of competitions, and so on. The managerial system must generally facilitate the coach's endeavors. This is done by providing support services and by serving as a liaison with external agents such as other national sport organizations, agencies that control facilities, government agencies, and travel agencies. The institutional system would, of course, be concerned with the larger issues of total finances, and support from the society and government. This is the ideal prescription for the operation of national teams. But, in practice, these principles are often disregarded. For example, individuals who are elected to the Board of Directors are often former athletes and/or club representatives. Thus, all their skills, capacities, and orientations may be most strongly related to the internal operations of the organization including the selection and operation of the national team. Conversely, they may not have the capacity or inclination to deal with external groups. If this is the case, it is not surprising to see considerable confusion and conflict in the management of the team.

Technical Core
in Service Organizations

Both Thompson and Parsons argued that the the technical core of an organization must be insulated from environmental disturbances. But their models overlooked one significant factor relating to service organizations —the interface between the customer and the employee. It was emphasized in Chapter 2 that the customer-employee interface differentiates service organizations from organizations that produce goods. While the notion of insulating the technical core is most meaningful and most practical in organizations producing goods, it may not be appropriate or practical in the case of service organizations. This is certainly the case in those organizations which depend on their employees to seek and recruit more customers from among a larger population. In many service organizations, employees who belong to the technical core (which, according to theory, should be insulated) are expected to interact with the public in the provision of their services, and in the recruitment of more customers. Consider, for example, the intramural department in a university. Its major purpose is to provide recreational opportunities for all the students on the campus. Consequently, it organizes various competitions and instructional classes in as many activities as possible. The task of managing these various programs is left to paid and/or volunteer leaders. They are, in essence, the employees who provide the services. But, their effectiveness is related not only to their ability to provide quality service but also in their ability to interact with and recruit from the student population. That is, the boundary spanning activities relating to both the current and prospective customers are left to the technical core employees. Thus, the notion of insulating the technical core appears to be irrelevant in the context of the intramural department and other similar service organizations. Yet, from another perspective, it is apparent that the departmental chairpersons and their assistants do shield the technical core from some of the environmental segments. For example, in matters relating to other academic departments, the Board of Governors, the physical plant, and so on, it is the managerial system which acts as the buffer. This partial insulation from some segments of the environment and openness to relevant publics in the immediate task environment is illustrated in Exhibit 4.8.

Exhibit 4.8. Technical Core in Service Organizations.

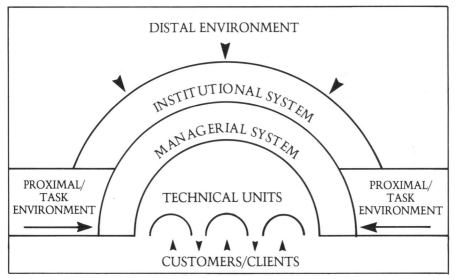

Structure of Authority in Service Organizations

It has also been pointed out that the conventional notions of a hierarchy of authority may not be meaningful in the context of service organizations, particularly the professional service organizations described in Chapter 2. As indicated previously, the raw material for a professional service organization is primarily knowledge and information. The processing of that information is the fundamental task of the employees. In so far as customers are unique and the problems that they bring to the interface are also highly variable, the customer-employee interface in a professional service organization operates in a highly unpredictable environment. Further, because they possess expertise and have direct access to relevant information, the professional employee must be given the freedom and right to make decisions regarding what type of services should be produced, how these should be produced, and how the service should be delivered.

Noting the unique properties of professional service organizations, Mills, Hall, Leidecker and Margulies (1983) have proposed a structural model for these organizations - the *flexiform*. The essence of the flexiform model is that the *operational units* (which are conceptually similar to the technical subsystem discussed earlier) and the *administrative core* (the managerial subsystem) are loosely coupled to each other.

The operational units are those involving the professionals and their customers. Each unit may consist of one professional or a team of professionals interacting with their customers. For example, each professor and his/her students in a faculty of physical education would constitute an operational unit. Viewed from a different perspective, the professors in the undergraduate program make up a team of experts interacting with a group of students. In this case, the undergraduate program is the operational unit.

According to Mills et al. (1983), these operational units "need to be basically self-contained, relatively autonomous units and essentially to operate as mini-companies; the service is being produced and delivered concurrently" (p. 125). Thus, a professor is given the autonomy and responsibility to design and teach a course(s), and decide on the evaluation system to be used. Further, the professor is also entitled to deal with each student according to the student's needs and abilities.

Mills et al. (1983) pointed out that the functions of the administrative core include setting broad policies, controlling the boundary conditions, linking and coordinating the activities of the operational units, and systematizing routine activities. In the example of the faculty of physical education, the chairperson, the dean , and the business managers, if any, would be the management team. Their function would be to mediate and coordinate among the various professors and their operational units (the course or groups of courses, and various research laboratories).

The idea of loosely coupled systems in the flexiform model stems from the distinction made by Mills et al. between *authority and functional power*. The concept of authority, as perceived by Mills et al., is conceptually similar to the concept of bureaucratic authority as perceived by Weber (1947). It refers to the right of superiors to make decisions which affect all subordinates of the organization. In the case of a faculty of physical education, the dean and other administrators have the authority to decide on the budget allocations to the professors and their labs, and on their teaching assignments. In contrast, functional power emerges from the expertise of the professional and the exigencies of the situation faced by the professional. Thus, as noted before, each of the **professors** in a faculty of physical education has the functional power to decide on the course content and methods of teaching and evaluation.

Simply stated, authority relates to decisions that affect all units (or most of them), and resides in the administrative core. Functional power relates to what happens within individual units, and stems from the expertise residing in the units. In the flexiform model (see Exhibit 4.9), functional power is greatest at the operational unit level. It decreases as it moves toward the administrative core at the center. Conversely, authority resides in the administrative core and flows toward the outer operational units.

In the context of a faculty of physical education, the professors have the functional power to make decisions over the processes in their respective operational units while the chairpersons and the dean have the authority to make decisions affecting the whole faculty.

Exhibit 4.9. Authority and Power Flows in Professional Service Organizations.
Adapted from: Mills, Etal., 1983.

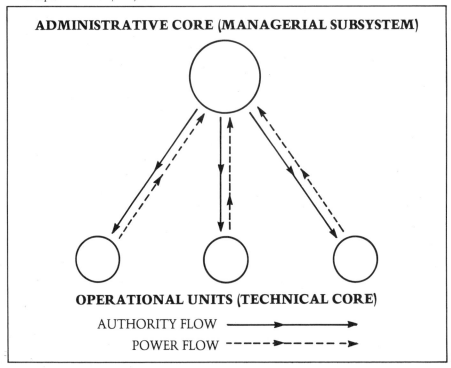

ADMINISTRATIVE CORE (MANAGERIAL SUBSYSTEM)

OPERATIONAL UNITS (TECHNICAL CORE)

AUTHORITY FLOW ——————▶

POWER FLOW – – – – – ▶ – – – – – ▶

Summary

In this chapter, the principles of organizing arising from Weber's (1947) concept of a bureaucracy, and from the open systems perspectives of Lawrence and Lorsch (1967), Thompson (1967), and Parsons (1960) were described. The relevance of these models to service organizations, particularly to sport organizations, was also highlighted. Particular emphasis was placed on the need to differentiate the subsystems of an organization.

Questions for Discussion

1. Describe a critical experience you have had with a bureaucracy in terms of both the positive and negative aspects of that experience.

2. To what degree are the programs (graduate, undergraduate, athletic, and/or intramural) in your university or college bureaucratized? What changes, if any, would you make in the administrative structure of these programs? Why?

3. Select one sport organization of your choice and define and describe the "technical core" of that organization. To what extent is that technical core protected from the external environment? How is this insulation of the technical core achieved?

References

Behling, O., & Schriesheim, C. (1976). Organizational behavior: Theory, research, and application. Boston: Allyn and Bacon,Inc.

Bell, E.C. (1974). A college of business administration as a productive system. Academy of Management Journal, 17, 306-317.

Blau, P.M. (1956). Bureaucracy in modern society. New York: Random House.

Cannel, M., Brittain, D., Howells, B., & Wright, P. (producers), & Brittain, D. (Director). (1979). Paperland [Film]. Ottawa: National Film Board of Canada.

Chelladurai, P. (1976). A composite production model for the degree programs in institutions of physical education. CAHPER Journal, 42, 30-35.

Filley, A.C., House, R.J., & Kerr, S. (1976). Managerial process and organizational behavior. Glenview, Ill.: Scott, Foresman and Company.

Fink, S.L., Jenks, R.S., & Willits, R.D. (1983).Designing and managing organizations. Homewood, Ill.: Richard D. Irwin, Inc.

Frisby, W.M. (1983). The organizational structure and effectiveness of Canadian national sport governing bodies. Unpublished doctoral dissertation, University of Waterloo, Waterloo, Canada.

Hoy, W.K., & Miskel, C.G. (1982). Educational administration. New York: Random House.

Keating, J.W. (1964). Sportsmanship as a moral category. Ethics, 75, 25-35.

Lawrence, P.R., & Lorsch, J.W. (1967). Differentiation and integration in complex organizations. Administrative Science Quarterly, 12, 1-47.

Mills, P.K., Hall, J.L., Leidecker, J.K., & Margulies, N. (1983). Flexiform: A model for professional service organizations. Academy of Management Review, 8, 118-131.

Mintzberg, H. (1979). The Structuring of organizations. Englewood Cliffs, N.J.: Prentice-Hall, Inc.

Parsons, T. (1960). Structure and process in modern societies. New York: The Free Press of Glencoe.

Perrow, C. (1972). Complex organizations: A critical essay. Glenview, Ill.: Scott, Foresman and Company.

Robbins, S.P. (1976). The administrative process: Integrating theory and practice. Englewood Cliffs, N.J.: Prentice-Hall, Inc.

Sofer, S. (1972). Organizations in theory and practice. New York: Basic Books, Inc.

Thompson, J.D. (1967). Organizations in action. New York: McGraw-Hill Book Compnay.

Weber, M. (1947). The theory of social and economic organization. (translated by A. M. Henderson and T. Parsons). New York: Oxford University Press.

Weber, M. (1958). From Max Weber: Essays in sociology. (Edited by Gerth, H.H., & Mills, C.W.). New York: Oxford University Press

CHAPTER 5

LEADING: MOTIVATIONAL BASIS

NEED BASED (OR CONTENT) THEORIES
      The Need Hierarchy Theory
      The ERG Theory
      The Two-Factor Theory
      The Task as a Motivator

PROCESS THEORIES
      Vroom's Expectancy Theory
      Adams' Theory of Inequity
      The Porter and Lawler Model of Motivation

SUMMARY

QUESTIONS FOR DISCUSSION

REFERENCES

After defining the goals for the organization and specifying the ways of achieving those goals (i.e., planning), and after clarifying who should do what (i.e., organizing), it becomes necessary for managers to motivate their subordinates to carry out their assignments so that the goals can be achieved (i.e., leading). While the planning and organizing functions require more of the technical and conceptual skills, the leading function is based on the human skills (see Chapter 1). Further, while the planning and organizing functions can be carried out without a great deal of interpersonal interaction with members, the leading function entails considerable face to face interactions with members — either collectively or individually. If managers are to be effective as leaders, they should have a clear understanding of how individuals are motivated, and what factors influence such motivation. While such insights into an understanding of member motivation can be gained through personal experience, it is also useful to consider the theories of motivation which have been advanced for an organizational context. Thus, some of the more relevant theories of work motivation are presented in this chapter.

It must be noted that since human behavior is highly variable, and individual differences in terms of needs and personality are numerous, none of the theories discussed in this chapter serves as a single framework that can be applied in all circumstances. However, an understanding of these theories does provide the manager with a gestalt view of the intricacies and complexities of human motivation, as well as insight into the appropriateness of the theories to specific situations. Further, although the various theories have a more direct bearing on the leading function, their relevance to the planning, organizing, and evaluating functions is also important.

What is motivation in the context of leading? Hoy and Miskel (1982) have defined it as "the complex forces, drives, needs, tension states, or other mechanisms that start and maintain voluntary activity toward the achievement of personal goals" (p. 137). They also expanded and stated that:

> Activating forces are assumed to exist within individuals. Examples of such internal forces include memory, affective responses, and pleasure-seeking tendencies. Motivation also directs or channels behavior; that is, it provides a goal orientation. Individual behavior is directed toward something. (p. 137)

In general, motivated behavior is thought of as behavior directed toward the fulfillment of a need, motive, or desire that has been deprived. Behavior is also influenced by an individual's experience with, and expectations for the consequences of such behavior.

Need Based (or Content) Theories

The general paradigm for motivational theories based on needs is that when a need is deprived, the individual is aroused and driven to seek the sources for the satisfaction of that need, and to take some action to achieve such satisfaction. The need based theories are also called "content" theories because they indicate what (i.e., content) motivates individuals to engage in specific behaviors.

While it is appropriate to state that needs underlie every action, there is some question about which of the numerous needs is most important in the determination of behavior. Does one need take precedence over another when two needs are deprived? Is there one class of needs that are predominant in influencing behavior? These are the types of questions addressed by various content theories of motivation. Three of the prominent theories — Maslow's Need Hierarchy Theory, Alderfer's Existence, Relatedness, and Growth (ERG) Theory, and Herzberg's Two-Factor Theory — are considered to be most relevant to the organizational context.

The Need Hierarchy Theory

The essence of Maslow's (1943) Need Hierarchy Theory lies in its specification of five classes of needs which are ordered in a hierarchy of prepotency (i.e., power or force). After stating that only unsatisfied needs are the basis of behavior and that satisfied needs lose their potency to instigate behavior, Maslow argued that people focus on meeting their basic needs and then move up the scale of the hierarchy of needs when the lower order (prepotent) needs are satisfied. In a commentary on the concept of a hierarchy of needs, Maslow (1943) stated that:

> It is quite true that man lives by bread alone — when there is no bread. But what happens to man's desires when there **is** plenty of bread and when his belly is chronically filled? **At once other (and 'higher') needs emerge** and these, rather than physiological hungers, dominate the organism. And when these in turn are satisfied, again new (and still 'higher') needs emerge and so on. This is what we mean by saying that the basic human needs are organized into a hierarchy of relative prepotency. (p. 375)

Maslow proposed five categories of needs in order of importance to the individual — *physiological, safety and security, love and belonging, esteem,* and *self-actualization needs.*

Physiological needs. Physiological needs relate to the more fundamental and biological requirements of a human being; e.g., food and shelter, and the need to avoid pain. Maslow felt that:

> these physiological needs are the most prepotent of all needs. What this means specifically is, that in the human being who is missing everything in life in an extreme fashion, it is most likely that the major motivation would be the physiological needs rather than any others. (p. 373)

From an organizational perspective, then, the employee must be provided with sufficient financial rewards (e.g., salary, bonus) to insure that the physiological needs are satisfied.

Safety and security needs. These needs refer to an individual's preference for "a safe, orderly, predictable, organized world, which he can count on, and in which unexpected, unmanageable or other dangerous things do not happen" (Maslow, 1943; p. 378). The safety and security needs, in essence, reflect a guarantee for tomorrow. That is, individuals want to be assured that what they enjoy now in terms of food and shelter will also be available in the future. This need for a safe and secure life is expressed through "such phenomena as ... the common preference for a job with tenure and protection, the desire for a savings account, and for insurance of various kinds (medical, dental, unemployment, disability, old age)" (Maslow, 1943; p. 379). In an organizational context, job security, health coverage, and retirement schemes are related to security needs while safe working conditions, precautions against accidents, and other such organizational efforts are aimed at satisfying the safety needs of employees.

Love needs. Love needs represent the desires of people for friendship and warm interpersonal interaction with others — to be associated with and accepted by others. It must be noted that these social needs enhance the survival potential of the species since humans can function better and achieve more in groups than as individuals. These needs become dominant only after the former two sets of needs — physiological needs and safety and security needs — are minimally satisfied. The satisfaction of the social needs in an organization is dependent upon the employee's coworkers, work groups, supervisors, and the intensity of their social needs.

Esteem needs. Esteem needs are considered to be higher order needs that relate to a person's desire to be recognized by others and to have status among them. According to Maslow, the esteem needs include a desire for strength, achievement, adequacy, confidence (self-esteem), recognition, and respect (esteem) from others. The title and status accorded to individuals in an organization, and the respect with which they are treated by peers are the kinds of factors that cater to esteem needs.

Self-actualization. Finally, at the highest level in Maslow's hierarchy is the need for self-actualization. Individuals operating at this level endeavor to be what they can be. Maslow (1943) suggested that:

> A musician must make music, an artist must paint, a poet must write, if he is to be ultimately happy. What a man **can** be, he **must** be. This need we may call self-actualization... It refers to the desire for self-fulfillment, namely, to the tendency for him to become actualized in what he is potentially. This tendency might be phrased as the desire to become more and more what one is, to become everything that one is capable of becoming. (p. 382)

Maslow felt that people who have satisfied their self-actualization need will provide the fullest and healthiest creativeness. He also acknowledged that such people are the exceptions rather than the rule.

One important component of Maslow's theory is often overlooked. Conventionally, the deprivation of a need is seen as the driving force, and scant attention is given to the effects of gratification of that need. In Maslow's theory, gratification of a need is as important as deprivation, because gratification releases the organism from one set of needs and activates another set. The process of the deprivation of a need dominating the individual, and its gratification activating the next higher level need is illustrated in Exhibit 5.1.

The notion of the hierarchy of the prepotency of needs is illustrated in the following example. A recent physical education graduate might be offered a position in a distant location. In order of priority (prepotency), the graduate will be concerned with salary and availability of housing (physiological needs); job security, safety of the prospective residential area, and the working conditions — particularly those relating to the equipment that the individual will have to use (safety and security needs); and type of coworkers and neighbors — their personality and their interpersonal orientation (social needs). After visits and interviews, the graduate might be reasonably confident that these needs would be satisfied, and consequently, would accept the job and work hard at it. After a period of time, superiors might recognize the effective performance of the individual and reward him/her with a promotion and an increase in salary. The graduate would be highly satisfied and would continue to work diligently and obtain the rewards and recognition associated with good performance. But after a number of years, however, a restlessness might develop. The graduate might feel that his/her personal abilities and personality require a different and more challenging task involving innovativeness and creativity (self-actualizing needs). So the graduate might leave the job for further education in the same or some other field.

Maslow viewed the classification of the needs as general in nature. However, he was the first to acknowledge that individual differences in

Exhibit 5.1. Maslow's Hierarchy of Needs.

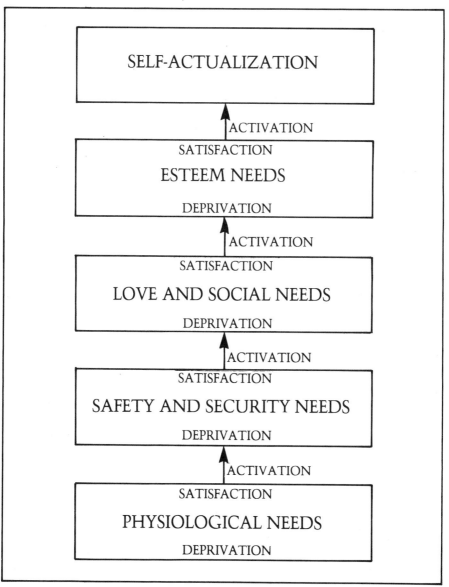

personality and experience might make the hierarchy of needs irrelevant in some cases. For instance, individuals who have been deprived of a lower order need for any length of time might either "fixate" at that level even after gratification of that need, or they might "renounce" that need and focus on a higher need. It is also possible that for some individuals, self-esteem might become prepotent even before the satisfaction of the love and social needs. In innately creative people, creativeness would supercede all other needs. And in some others, "the level of aspiration may be permanently deadened or lowered. That is to say, the less prepotent goals may be lost, and may disappear forever, so that the person who has experienced life at a very low level, i.e., chronic unemployment, may continue to be satisfied for the rest of his life if only he can get enough food" (Maslow, 1943, p. 386).

Maslow also emphasized that the notion of a hierarchy of needs does not imply that one set of needs has to be fulfilled completely before another set becomes potent. In fact, "a more realistic description of the hierarchy would be in terms of decreasing percentages of satisfaction as we go up the hierarchy of prepotency" (Maslow, 1943, p. 388). That is, the average person experiences greater percentages of satisfaction of the lower order needs (physiological, security, and love needs) while much smaller percentages of the higher order needs are satisfied.

One major limitation of Maslow's theory is that it cannot be adequately tested. Because individuals progress through the hierarchy of needs one at a time, it could take a life time for some individuals to reach the highest level (i.e., self-actualization). Thus, it becomes inconvenient, if not impossible, to test the theory — data would have to be collected over the lifetime of subjects. A second limitation of the theory is also associated with difficulties in measurement. There is also a possibility that one set of behaviors could result in the satisfaction of more than one set of needs. For example, when a faculty member engages in research and produces quality publications, it might result in the award of tenure (security), recognition by colleagues (esteem), and a sense of achievement and growth (self-actualization). There is no acceptable way of determining which of these was prepotent.

Although the theory is not readily subject to empirical research, it does have an intuitive appeal[1] — particularly from a managerial perspective in terms of the emphasis placed on needs. As Fink, Jenks and Willits(1983) pointed out, the theory "provides a few simple, direct, and useful categories for sorting out a wide range of specific needs, it has an established history of application to organizations, and, ... it provides a basis for judging the effectiveness of a reward system" (p. 123).

1. Alderman (1974) has speculated that an individual's activity preferences could be related to Maslow's hierarchy of needs. Activities like hunting and fishing could reflect the physiological needs in primitive cultures. Alderman also cited the example of Eskimo children who prefer cooperative games to competitive games. These preferences could be a reflection of survival needs. It was also suggested that people operating at the level of safety needs would prefer predictable, and safe and secure sports like golf. The love and social needs also could be the basis for participation of many people. The dedication and perseverance with which individuals take to an activity could very well reflect their concern for self-esteem. It could also be possible for individuals to self-actualize in sport — they become one with the sport. Finally, Alderman suggested that "games and sports events reflecting the higher order needs would exhibit more variability, originality, and creativity" (p. 169).

The ERG Theory

One notable attempt to modify Maslow's theory, in light of the limitations discussed above was Alderfer's (1972) *ERG Theory*. Alderfer proposed that needs can be classified into three broad categories — *Existence, Relatedness,* and *Growth* (and, thus, the acronym ERG). As the name implies, Existence needs refer to everything needed to insure continued existence. In that sense, the existence needs are similar to Maslow's physiological needs. Relatedness is associated with the individual's need to interact with others and share their feelings and thoughts. And, finally, Growth is related to the need to achieve in challenging tasks and to develop new capacities and creativity.

Although these three categories of needs can be generally viewed as simply a collapsing or condensing of Maslow's five levels of needs, there are some significant differences in the type of needs included in the categories. Alderfer distinguished between two types of safety needs — those that relate to material objects in the work place, and those that relate to people. The material based safety needs are classified with the physiological needs under Existence, while the people related safety needs are included in the category of Relatedness. The second difference relates to the esteem needs. Esteem from others, according to Alderfer, belongs to the Relatedness category while self-esteem belongs to the Growth category.

The basis for Alderfer's three level categorization of needs is that the targets toward which needs are directed are different, and, therefore, the processes for satisfying those needs are also different. Hoy and Miskel (1982) elaborated on this point:

> *Material objects are the targets of existence needs, and the process of getting enough is the means to satisfy the needs. Significant others are the targets of relatedness needs, and the process of mutuality is the means to satisfy those needs. Particular environments or settings are the targets of growth needs, and the process of individual differentiation and integration is the means to satisfy the need for growth. (p. 144)*

Despite these differences between Maslow's five-level hierarchy and the ERG theory, it is reasonable to consider the latter as a modification of the former. Alderfer himself has acknowledged that he was considerably influenced by Maslow's work. The similarities and differences between the two models are illustrated in Exhibit 5.2.

The Two-Factor Theory

While Maslow and Alderfer felt that even the lower order needs could serve as motivators when they were deprived, Herzberg and his associates (Herzberg, Mausner, and Snyderman, 1959; Herzberg, 1968) contended that the

Exhibit 5.2. Comparison of Maslow's and Alderfer's Theories.

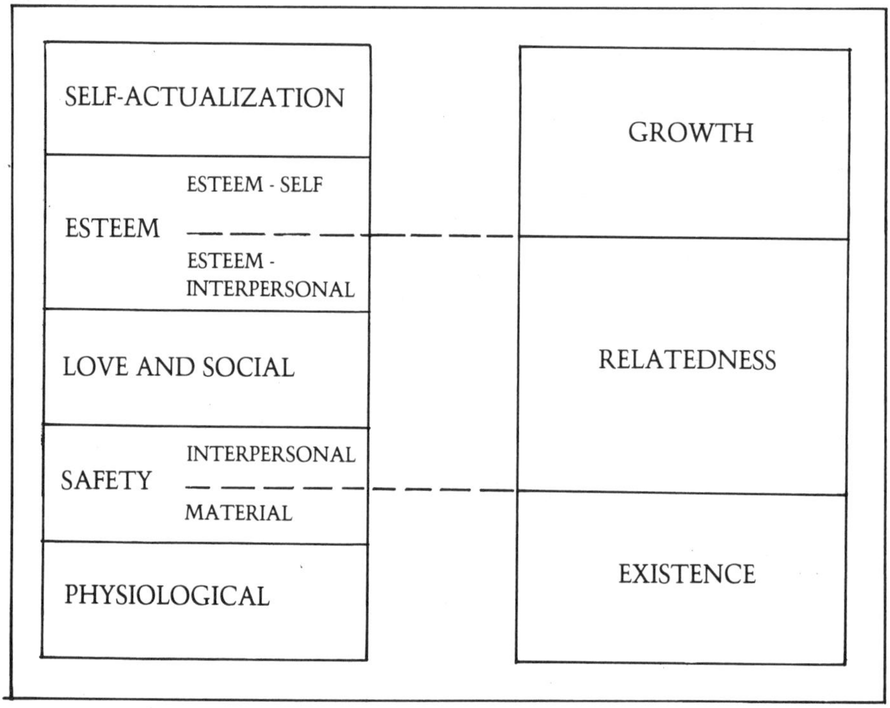

SELF-ACTUALIZATION	GROWTH
ESTEEM ESTEEM - SELF / ESTEEM - INTERPERSONAL	
LOVE AND SOCIAL	RELATEDNESS
SAFETY INTERPERSONAL / MATERIAL	
PHYSIOLOGICAL	EXISTENCE

two sets of needs (higher order and lower order needs) are associated with satisfaction and dissatisfaction differentially. In contrast to the common view that satisfaction and dissatisfaction are two polar extremes on one continuum, Herzberg considered them to be on two separate continua. Herzberg (1968) explained that:

> The factors involved in producing job satisfaction (and motivation) are separate and distinct from the factors that lead to job dissatisfaction. Since separate factors need to be considered, depending on whether job satisfaction or job dissatisfaction is being examined, it follows that these two feelings are not opposites of each other. The opposite of job satisfaction is not job dissatisfaction, rather **no** job satisfaction; and, similarly, the opposite of job dissatisfaction is not job satisfaction, but **no** job dissatisfaction. (p. 56)

The fundamental postulate of the theory is that only higher order needs affect satisfaction while the lower order needs are associated with dissatisfaction. As a consequence, Herzberg's theory is called a two-factor (or dual factor) theory. In order to understand the theory better, it is useful to examine how it evolved.

In their analysis of previous research results, Herzberg and his colleagues could not find any consistent results that would relate needs to motivation. They also felt that the available research supported a conclusion that different classes of needs are differentially associated with satisfaction or motivation. In order to test this proposition, they interviewed and administered a semi-structured questionnaire to approximately two hundred engineers and accountants. The questionnaire required the respondents to think back to one incident in their work when they had felt extremely happy and satisfied, and to another incident when they had felt extremely unhappy and dissatisfied. They were also asked to indicate what effects these feelings of happiness had had on their subsequent work and how long these feelings lasted. The content of the responses were then analyzed, and sixteen factors were identified as the causes of satisfaction or dissatisfaction. The data analyses showed that one set of factors (called the *satisfiers* or *motivators*) was cited more often in reference to satisfaction than to dissatisfaction. Another set (called the *dissatisfiers* or *hygienes*) was referred to more often in incidents of dissatisfaction than of satisfaction. As mentioned previously, all of the satisfiers or motivators were related to higher order needs while the dissatisfiers were associated with lower order needs. In Exhibit 5.3, the composite of the results of this and twelve other subsequent research studies is presented.

The most important product of Herzberg's work was the finding that the motivators (or growth factors) were all related to the *content* of the work itself, while the hygiene factors were all related to the *context* in which the work was carried out. The content factors are achievement, recognition for achievement, the work itself, responsibility, and growth or advancement. The contextual factors are company policy and administration, supervision, interpersonal relationships, working conditions, salary, status, and security.

On the basis of his research findings, Herzberg concluded that management must be concerned with eliminating dissatisfaction by improving the hygiene factors — providing adequate salary and wages, good working conditions, and having meaningful company policies and quality supervision. But, he also pointed out that these hygiene factors alone do not result in motivated or satisfied workers. Management, must also change jobs in order to provide for the psychological growth of employees.

This process of *job enrichment* is the practical application of Herzberg's theory.[2] Job enrichment (or *vertical job loading* as it is also called) involves redesigning jobs so that employees experience the higher order needs. Some of

2. Rees (1980) has argued that the concept of job enrichment should be applied to sport, particularly team sports. In this context, "the desires and goals of the individual athlete are deemed important and catering for the 'I' in the 'team' provides the key to motivation" (p. 30). It would be worthwhile to conduct research to find out if job enrichment does contribute to athletes' satisfaction as well as to their performance.

the ways in which this can be accomplished, according to Herzberg (1968), are to assign whole units of work to employees (rather than having different employees responsible for different segments), to remove or reduce control and supervision, to grant additional authority, and to increase the difficuly of the tasks assigned.

Exhibit 5.3. Satisfaction and Dissatisfaction as a Function of Two Separate Sets of Factors.

Adapted from Herzberg, 1968.

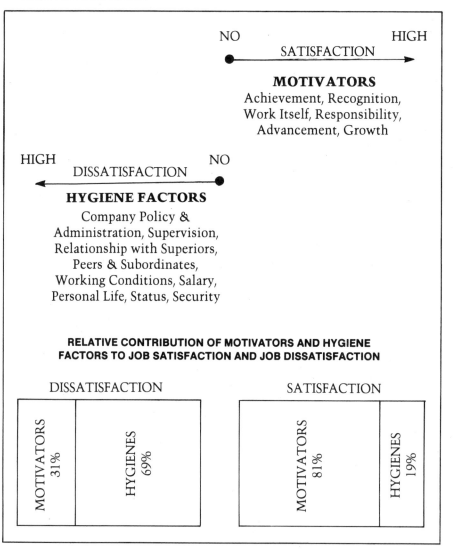

RELATIVE CONTRIBUTION OF MOTIVATORS AND HYGIENE FACTORS TO JOB SATISFACTION AND JOB DISSATISFACTION

The two-factor theory is, perhaps, the most controversial theory of work motivation. There are two serious criticisms which detract from the usefulness of this theory. First, although two distinct sets of factors are assumed to influence satisfaction and dissatisfaction, Herzberg's data did not completely support this assumption. Many of the same conditions contributed to both satisfaction and dissatisfaction. For example, although it has been suggested that the hygiene factors exclusively influence job dissatisfaction, in Herzberg's research, 31 per cent of all the factors contributing to job dissatisfaction were motivators (see Exhibit 5.3). Similarly, although it was suggested that the motivators exclusively influence job satisfaction, 19 per cent of all the factors contributing to job satisfaction were hygiene factors. In short, there are individual differences in the manner and extent to which the hygiene and motivator factors affect different people. However, Herzberg's emphasis on the generality of the impact of each category or factor overlooked or minimized such individual differences.

The second criticism relates to the methodology used by Herzberg and his associates. The respondents were asked to recall incidents in which they felt satisfied or dissatisfied —an approach known as the *critical incident method.* But, when individuals are asked to recall incidents and express their reactions to them, they tend to attribute all the positive or happy events to their own efforts and achievements. Conversely, all negative outcomes are assigned to some external agent like company policy, supervision, and so on. This is a defensive mechanism individuals use to protect their image and self-esteem. As Vroom (1964) stated:

Persons may be more likely to attribute the causes of satisfaction to their own achievements and accomplishments on the job. On the other hand, they may be more likely to attribute their dissatisfaction not to personal inadequacies or deficiencies, but to factors in the work environment, i.e., obstacles presented by company policies or supervision. (p. 129)

Studies that have attempted to use other methods have found that Herzberg's theory was not supported by the results (e.g., Dunnette, Campbell, and Hakel, 1967; Hulin and Smith, 1967). Consequently, it has been suggested that the two-factor theory is limited by the method used to develop it.

The motivators in the motivation-hygiene theory are similar to Maslow's higher order needs, and to Alderfer's growth needs. But, this is where the similarity to the the other two theories ends. As noted previously, while both Maslow and Alderfer contended that even the lower order needs can motivate workers, Herzberg stated that only the factors intrinsic to the job can serve as motivators.

Despite this difference, all three theories have one general implication for management. That is, management should be concerned with making work meaningful for the workers. This viewpoint is in contrast with the classical and bureaucratic approaches which emphasized the fractionation of work (resulting in narrow routine and monotonous jobs) to ensure efficiency and productivity. Further, earlier approaches which emphasized uniformity and consistency of operation, tended to impose rules and procedures which governed the activities of the workers. These two aspects of the classical approach to management are not conducive to the pursuit or fulfillment of higher order needs.

The Task as a Motivator

The interest generated by the Maslow, Alderfer, and Herzberg theories in the job and its content lead some researchers to focus on the motivational properties of the task. It was noted earlier that Herzberg proposed a set of guidelines for "enriching" jobs. A number of other scholars (e.g., Hackman, 1969; Hackman and Oldham, 1976; 1980; Scott, 1966; Steers, 1975; Turner and Lawrence,1965) have studied the attributes of jobs and the effects of such attributes on employee attitudes, satisfaction and productivity. The model presented by Hackman and Oldham (1980) is perhaps the most comprehensive. Also, it provides a framework to analyze the tasks, the people, and the fit between the two. The Hackman and Oldham *job characteristics model*, illustrated in Exhibit 5.4, is based on the assumption that certain characteristics of a job enhance the psychological states of the workers. In turn, these psychological states are associated with internal motivation, satisfaction, and performance.

The critical psychological states that enhance internal motivation toward work are *knowledge of results, experienced responsibility,* and *experienced meaningfulness of the work.* Unless the individual knows how well (or poorly) the job has been performed, there is no basis to feel satisfied or dissatisfied about performance or to adjust personal aspirations and efforts. Thus, the knowledge of results represents a key factor in internal motivation.

The second psychological state underlying internal work motivation is the perception of personal responsibility — when the individual feels largely responsible for the successful completion of a task. To the extent that personal responsibility is reduced, the internal motivation is likely to be negatively affected.

The third, and final psychological state in the Hackman and Oldham model is the experienced meaningfulness of the work. That is, "the person must *experience the work as meaningful,* as something that 'counts' in one's system of values" Hackman and Oldham, 1980, p. 73).

According to Hackman and Oldham, it is necessary for all three of the above factors to be present for high internal work motivation to develop and persist. As an illustration of this, Hackman and Oldham (1980) cited the example of golf:

> It is ironic that the three psychological states often characterize games played for pleasure better than they do work in organizations. Consider, for example, the game of golf. Knowledge of results is direct and immediate; the player hits the ball and sees at once where it goes .... Experienced personal responsibility for the outcomes also is clear and high, despite the tendency of the golfers sometimes to claim that the slice was due to someone whispering behind the tee .... Experienced meaningfulness also is high, despite the fact that the task itself is mostly devoid of cosmic significance .... So, in golf, the three psychological states are present, and internal motivation among regular golfers is usually quite high. Indeed, golfers exhibit an intensity of behavior that is rarely seen in the workplace; getting up before dawn to be first on the tee, feeling jubilation or despair all day depending on how well the morning round was played, sometimes even destroying the tools and equipment —not out of boredom or frustration with the work (as is sometimes seen in the industrial settings) but rather from anger at oneself for not playing better. (p. 74-75)

A major supposition in Hackman and Oldham's theory is that these psychological states can be cultivated by designing jobs in order to include the significant characteristics of *skill variety, task identity, task significance, autonomy,* and *feedback.*

Skill variety. Skill variety refers to "the degree to which a job requires a variety of different activities in carrying out the work, involving the use of a number of different skills and talents of the person" (Hackman and Oldham, 1980, p. 78). Thus, a teacher who teaches a number of sports to different classes of students, coaches the school basketball team, and, in addition, counsels problem students experiences more variety in the job than a teacher who teaches one activity to various classes of students. Speculating that "the link between skill variety and experienced meaningfulness is probably 'wired in' for human organisms" (Hackman and Oldham, 1980, p. 78), the authors stated that a job can be meaningful to workers if it utilizes their skills and talents, and develops them further.

Task identity. Task identity refers to "the degree to which a job requires completion of a 'whole' and identifiable piece of work, that is, doing a job from beginning to end with a visible outcome" (Hackman and Oldham, 1980, p. 78). This concept is antithetical to the notion of division of work — the fractionation of job(s) into specific activities to be carried out by different individuals; e.g., an automobile assembly line.

Exhibit 5.4. Hackman and Oldham's Job Characteristics Model.

Reproduced with permission from: Hackman, J.R. & Oldham, C.R. *Work Redisgn*, Reading, Mass.: Addision-Wesley Publishing Company, 1980©, (p. 90).

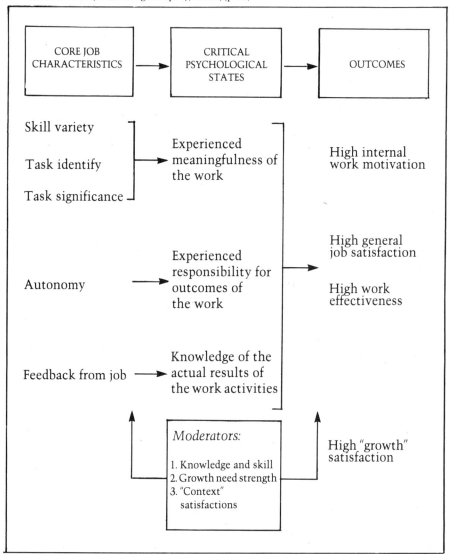

High task identity would be available to high school coaches. They develop the athletic potential of the few students who report for the team. This development is easily identified and, attributed to the coach who is usually the sole individual responsible for that task. In contrast, classroom teachers cannot easily identify their end product or their personal contributions to that end product. Hackman and Oldham suggested that a social worker who deals with all of the needs of a client will find the job more menaingful than one who deals with only one problem.

Task significance. The significance of the task reflects "the degree to which a job has a substantial impact on the lives of other people, whether those people are in the immediate organization or in the world at large" (Hackman and Oldham, 1980, p. 79). Teachers and coaches are aware that they are engaged in shaping the lives of their students, and, in turn, the future of society. In contrast, school custodians are not likely to attribute the same level of significance to their jobs. "When we know that what we do in our work will affect someone else's happiness, health, or safety, we care about that work more than if the work is largely irrelevant to the lives and well-being of other people" (Hackman and Oldham, 1980, p. 79).

Although the importance of task significance may be self-evident, there are some unresolved issues associated with it. Neither Hackman and Oldham nor other researchers have commented on the possible distinction between significance that is personally experienced by an employee, and the significance attached to that job by other external agents. For example, other professionals know that the physical education teacher's job is significant. But, it is possible that in some situations, board members and the administrators of a school system, the principals, and possibly the parents might feel that a physical education teacher is simply "bouncing a ball and blowing a whistle". If low significance is attached to the domain and reflected in budget allocations, staffing practices, and so on, it may not be possible for a physical education teacher to maintain the personal conviction that the job is significant.

This same issue of personally felt significance versus attributed significance arises when the tasks of a teacher and a coach are compared. While there is no attempt here to evaluate these two jobs, it is obvious that the media and the community are likely to distort the relative significance of the two jobs. That is, the coaching job is likely to be treated as more significant than the teaching job.

In Hackman and Oldham's model, the three charactertistics of skill variety, task identify, and task significance contribute to the experienced meaningfulness of the task. All three characteristics do not have to be present for a worker to find the job meaningful. For instance, welders working on a large bridge could find their job very meaningful because it contributed to the safety of the bridge, and, consequently, to the safety of the public. Nonetheless, the job would rank very low in terms of skill variety and or task identity. Similarly, an individual who welds a wrought iron fence might find the task meaningful because all of the work, when finished, would represent a personal accomplishment.

Autonomy. Autonomy means "the degree to which the job provides substantial freedom, independence, and discretion to the individiual in scheduling the work and in determining the procedures to be used in carrying it out" (Hackman and Oldham, 1980, p. 79). In order for an individual to feel personally responsible and accountable in a job situation, the job should not be overly regulated by rules and procedures, manuals, and/or tight supervision.

Job feedback. Job feedback is "the degree to which carrying out the work activities provides the individual with direct and clear information about the effectiveness of his or her performance" (Hackman and Oldham, 1980, p. 80). Job feedback is different from the feedback provided by other agents such as a supervisor. In basketball shooting, for example, there is immediate feedback about the effectiveness of an attempt. That is, feedback is provided through the task itself. A coach may, however, point out that the attempt should (or should not) have been made depending on the particular game context. In the Hackman and Oldham model, the feedback mechanisms inherent in the job itself are emphasized.

As is illustrated in Exhibit 5.4, Hackman and Oldham proposed that a job possessing the characteristics of skill variety, task identity, and task significance will be associated with a perception that the job is meaningful. Similarly, when the worker is given the autonomy to decide the manner in which effort is expended, the perception of responsibility for the outcomes of the work increases. Finally, the feedback that is inherent in a job provides knowledge of the results of the work activities. According to Hackman and Oldham, the cumulative effects of these three critical psychological states positively influence the internal motivation of the employees, the quality of their work, and their satisfaction, and reduce the rates of absenteeism and turnover.

The final element in the job characteristics model is the moderating effects of individual differences (see Exhibit 5.4). That is, the relationship between the job characteristics on the one hand and internal motivation, satisfaction, and performance on the other is dependent on an individual's knowledge and skills, growth need strength, and satisfaction with other organizational factors. Lack of knowledge and skill (i.e., competency) at a task may be frustrating rather than motivating even if the job is high in motivating potential. Growth need strength refers to people's "strong needs for personal accomplishments, for learning, and for developing themselves beyond where they are now" (Hackman and Oldham, 1980, p. 85). Those who are low on this need to grow are less likely to be motivated by the job and its characteristics. The final individual difference factor referred to by Hackman and Oldham is an individual's satisfaction with other organizational factors like pay and job security. If there is great dissatisfaction with factors surrounding the job, then the job itself might lose its motivating potential.

In overview, Hackman and Oldham's job characteristics model is an extension of the content theories. However, it includes a greater emphasis on the job and the motivating potential of various characteristics of the job.

Process Theories

As noted earlier, the content theories are concerned with the factors that motivate the worker — personal factors like individual needs and/or organizational factors like the task assignment and rewards. But, they do not explain how individuals choose one behavior from the several open. The process theories of motivation deal with the individual's evaluation and choice of certain courses of action, and how other factors influence the outcomes of such courses of action. Three process models of motivation — Vroom's Expectancy Theory, Adams' Equity Theory, and Porter and Lawler's Model of Motivation — are presented in the following sections. These three models are considered to be most relevant to organizations.

Vroom's Expectancy Theory

The main postulate of expectancy theory is that individuals evaluate the various courses of action that are available to them, and choose the one that they expect to result in the outcomes they prefer. More explicitly, as Vroom (1964) stated:

The force on a person (motive) to perform a given act is based on the weighted value (or utility) of all the possible outcomes of the act multiplied by the perceived usefulness of the act in the attainment of these outcomes. Whenever an individual chooses between alternatives that involve certain outcomes, it seems clear that his behavior is affected not only by his preferences among outcomes, but also by the degree to which he believes these outcomes to be probable. (Vroom, 1964; p. 18)

Vroom's expectancy theory incorporates four major variables (or concepts) — *valence, outcome, expectancy,* and *instrumentality.*

Valence. An individual's preferences for particular outcomes is referred to as valence. If a particular outcome is very strongly preferred (e.g., a trade from one team to another in professional baseball), then the valence for the outcome would approach the value of +1. If, on the other hand, an outcome is strongly detested (e.g., transfer to a distant locality), then the valence would approach —1. According to the theory, the actual valence for the trade is based on the relative weighting of the positive and negative aspects of that outcome. Thus, a trade is a valued outcome but it entails a transfer to another place which is negatively valued. The degree to which the trade would be preferred would be indicated by the average value of the two outcomes (i.e., the trade and the transfer). When an individual is indifferent to a particular outcome, the valence is considered to be zero. Other terms that can be used to refer to the "valence" concept are incentives, rewards, or utility.

Outcomes. Outcomes refer to the consequences of a given act. For instance, an employee's promotion is an outcome. But this promotion is only a consequence of the employee having achieved certain performance standards set by the organization. Thus, there are two sets of outcomes which result from the efforts of the employee. Vroom calls these the first level and second level outcomes. The first level outcome refers to the performance standards achieved by the employee while the second level outcome refers to the rewards for that performance. It must also be noted that the *first level outcome is what the organization expects* (e.g., productivity) while the *second level outcomes are what the employee desires* (e.g., promotion, pay increase).

Expectancy. Expectancy is the probability estimate that effort will lead to the first level outcome — the performance standards set out by the organization. If, in the above example, the employee believed that his/her efforts would result in superior performance, then the expectancy would approach the value of +1. If, however, the employee felt that his/her capacities were not sufficient to reach that level of performance, then the expectancy would approach the value of zero. It must be noted that expectancy refers to the individual's *perception of the probability* that effort will lead to a standard of performance.

Instrumentality. The individual's estimate of the relationship between the first level outcomes and the second level outcomes is called instrumentality. If the employee in the above example believed that performing at a high level would automatically result in promotion, then instrumentality would approach the value of +1. If, however, the employee believed that promotion was based only on seniority and not on performance, then instrumentality would drop to zero. In contrast to expectancy which is *perceived probability,* instrumentality reflects the individual's *perception* that there is a good relationship between first level and second level outcomes. Expectancy connects individual effort to first level outcome while instrumentality links the first and second level outcomes. A coach might have a strong belief that if she recruits heavily her team will be successful (expectancy). She might also hold the strong belief that if her team is successful, she will receive a pay increase (instrumentality). The relationships among the above variables or concepts are illustrated in Exhibit 5.5.

It is assumed within Vroom's expectancy theory that the force (equated here with motivation) with which an individual engages in an activity is dependent upon the valence or attraction for the rewards or incentives the organization has to offer, the expectancy that effort results in a certain level of performance, and the instrumentality of such performance in the attainment of the rewards sought. This interplay of factors can be expressed as follows:

Force = Valence x Expectancy x Instrumentality

In this equation, the values for all of the variables on the right hand side of the equation must be positive and not equal to zero if the force is to be positive (i.e., if the individual is to be motivated). In simpler terms, if an individual dislikes an outcome (the valence is negative), there will be no motivation toward that outcome. If anything, the behavior aimed at avoiding that outcome will be motivated. Similarly, both expectancy and instrumentality must be non-zero. That is, the individual must believe that effort will ultimately result in the preferred rewards.

In overview, Vroom's model outlines relevant variables associated with motivated behavior and their interrelationships. More importantly, through the introduction of concepts such as valence, expectancy, and instrumentality, it helps to account for individual differences in motivated behavior.

Exhibit 5.5. Vroom's Expectancy Model of Motivation.

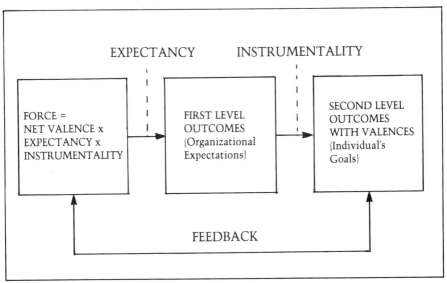

However, it does not provide any guidelines for the practicing manager. Furthermore, an assumption implicit in the model is that individuals behave in a rational manner. This is simply not the case. As was already noted in Chapter 3, individuals do not have the capacity to go through all the complicated calculations. Subsequent modifications of and extensions to Vroom's theory have improved its practical usefulness.

Adams' Theory of Inequity

While the content theories of Maslow and Herzberg emphasize the concept of "satisfaction", they are simplistic in their assumption that when a need is fulfilled, satisfaction automatically follows. From an organizational perspective, this is not necessarily true. For instance, when an individual is given a raise in pay, does it automatically lead to satisfaction? Or, does the person compare the raise to some standard and then experience satisfaction or dissatisfaction?

These issues were addressed by Adams (1963, 1977) in his Theory of Inequity. Basically, Adams stated that, on receipt of a reward, a person compares that reward to some internalized standard. If the comparison is favorable, then, there is satisfaction. If the comparison is unfavorable, however, there is dissatisfaction.

This phenomenon is quite common among students. It is not enough to receive a 'B' grade in a course. That grade must be comparable to what other students receive. Similarly, a merit raise of $1000 does not provide happiness in a professor if every other professor received $1001. The important point in both of these examples is that the absolute amount does not have a bearing on the estimation of equity; it is the relative amount that is critical.

The individual's internalized standard could be simply a comparison between personal effort (inputs) and the rewards of that effort (outcomes). For example, if great sacrifices are made in an effort to lose weight but only two pounds are lost in six months, the individual would have a feeling of inequity. This feeling would result from a simple comparison of personal cost versus personal benefit. But, in an organizational context, the cost-benefit comparison extends to referent others in the organization. That is, an individual compares the personal cost-benefit balance to the cost-benefit ratio of others in the work group. Adams' theory is anchored on this comparison to a referent other(s). As he noted:

> Inequity exists for **Person** (emphasis added) whenever he perceives that the ratio of his outcomes to inputs and the ratio of **Other's** (emphasis added) outcomes to Other's inputs are unequal. (Adams, 1977, p. 113)

The *other* in Adams' theory could be a subordinate, a supervisor, a coworker, or an employee in another comparable organization or occupation. It is also possible for an individual to compare the input/outcome balance of a current situation to that experienced in a previous one.

The concept of *inputs* in Adams' theory refers to the personal contributions for which the individual expects to receive a reward. Some of the factors that a person may consider as inputs are: intelligence, education and training, experience and seniority, personal appearance or attractiveness, health, and, effort on the job. *Outcomes* in an organizational context, include pay, seniority and other fringe benefits, working conditions including status and perquisites, and the psychological or intrinsic rewards of the job. Outcomes may also be negative as in the case of poor working conditions. Thus, the theory of inequity is based on an individual's perception of the balance between personal outcomes (benefits) and inputs (costs) relative to the outcomes and inputs of others.

There are three possible results of such comparisons — equity, inequity unfavorable to the individual (i.e., a referent's cost-benefit ratio is greater), and inequity favorable to the individual (i.e., the personal cost-benefit ratio is greater).

When a person perceives inequity, and feels the tension and discomfort associated with such inequity, an attempt may be made to restore equity (or reduce the inequity) in a number of ways. Obviously, the person may attempt to alter the values of any of the four elements of the inequity formula — *personal outcomes, personal inputs, other's outcomes,* and *other's inputs.* The most frequently used strategy is to attempt to increase personal outcomes. Thus, an individual is most likely to approach an employer and ask for more pay, greater benefits, and so on. If that approach fails, the individual may attempt to increase personal outcomes by putting in a greater number of hours and/or producing better quality work. It is also possible, of course, to reduce the feeling of inequity by reducing personal inputs through decreased productivity and/or increased absenteeism. Inequity could also be reduced by reducing other's outcomes or inputs. However, the individual may be constrained from adopting this strategy. Other's outcomes (i.e., pay, promotion) are most likely to be determined by superiors and other's inputs are most strongly influenced by that other individual. More importantly, a strategy which focuses on other's inputs or outcomes may not be psychologically acceptable to the person. Very few students could go to a professor and ask that the grade of another student be reduced. Also, very few students could destroy another student's class notes.

Although the theoretical possibility exists that inequity in favor of the individual may be experienced (e.g., received a higher pay raise than was deserved), individuals may not express a feeling of inequity as often (or as strongly) as they do when they perceive inequity of the opposite type. However, feelings of discomfort and guilt could arise. If this is the case, the individual is likely to put in greater efforts in an effort to justify the rewards received.

Apart from manipulating personal outcomes and inputs, there are other ways of reducing inequity. Adams suggested that individuals may alter their perceptions of personal and other's outcomes and inputs in such a manner that equity is perceptually restored. Or, a person may also change the other of comparison. Thus, a professor might believe that he had a productive year and, therefore, deserved a high merit increase. But, this perception could change if the total faculty's accomplishments were listed. Another possibility is that the professor could leave the situation and go elsewhere.

128

Although Adams indicated that the theory was relevant to any situation of social exchange (e.g., husband and wife, partners in tennis, and so on), he used the organizational context as the backdrop for the development of his theory. And, most of the examples listed in his writings relate to organizations and their members.

The significance of the Adams' theory lies in the fact that organizational reward systems are considered to be meaningful and effective only in so far as they create a sense of equity among the members of the organization. This notion is further elaborated on in the Porter and Lawler Model of Motivation.

The Porter and Lawler Model of Motivation

The model of motivation proposed by Porter and Lawler (1968) is an extension and elaboration of Vroom's expectancy theory, as well as a synthesis of both the content and process theories discussed previously. The model is schematically represented in Exhibit 5.6. In order to facilitate discussion of the model, numbers have been placed in the boxes in Exhibit 5.6.

Exhibit 5.6. The Porter-Lawler Model of Motivation.

Reproduced with permission from L.W. Porter and E.E. Lawler, *Managerial Attitudes and Performance,* Homewood, Ill.: Richard D. Irwin, Inc., 1968©, p. 165.

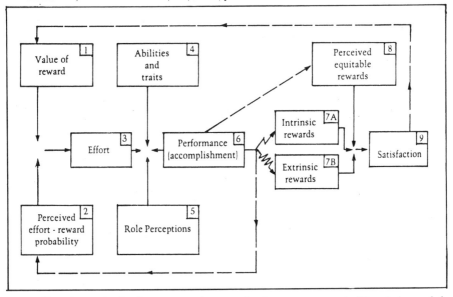

Effort (Box 3) which is equivalent to the force concept in Vroom's model, refers to the motivation behind an individual's effort in the work context. That is, the degree of effort expended is a reflection of an individual's motivational state. This motivation is a function of the value that the individual attaches to the possible rewards (Box 1), and the individual's perceptions of the probability that effort will result in reward (Box 2). It should be apparent that 'value of rewards' and 'perceived effort-reward probability' are equivalent to Vroom's concepts of 'valence' and 'expectancy' respectively. The effort expended by an employee results in certain level of performance (Box 6). Performance, in this context, refers to what is expected of the employee by the organization. That is, individuals may have their own standards of performance, but in an organization, performance is measured in terms of organizational standards, rules, expectations, and so on. Thus, a member of a faculty of physical education is expected to do an adequate job in teaching , research, and community work. The individual could do an outstanding job of coaching various community volleyball clubs but this would be of minimal value if teacher ratings were low and little research and writing were carried out.

One of the significant contributions of the Porter and Lawler model is that the complexity of the effort-performance relationship is highlighted. Effort does not always lead directly to good performance. For effective performance to occur, an individual must have the necessary abilities and traits (Box 4). Thus, a player who is five feet tall (which represents a "trait") cannot adequately perform in the position of a basketball center. Similarly, a person who is seven feet tall also would not be effective as a basketball center without any previous training (ability). It should be noted that while traits are enduring and stable characteristics, abilities are transient and trainable qualities.

Another factor that affects the effort-performance relationship is the accuracy of the individual's role perception (Box 5). Each employee must have a complete understanding of what activities are necessary and how they should be carried out. Thus, in the earlier example of the the physical education professor, time and effort would be required in course design and the preparation of lectures and examinations in order for the teaching function to be carried out effectively. As another example, marathon runners should not be involved in the same type of training as weight lifters. The role of a marathon runner requires cardiovascular endurance training, not strength training.

If the individual has the necessary abilities and traits, and perceives his/her role correctly, it is reasonable to expect that an acceptable level of performance (i.e., acceptable in terms of organizational expectations) will be accomplished. Such a performance will result in certain rewards. Intrinsic rewards (Box 7A) relate to the higher order needs of the individual. These rewards are personally derived from the accomplishments. That is, the individual receives a sense of achievement and experiences growth on the successful completion of a challenging task. In contrast to the intrinsic rewards which are personally derived, the extrinsic rewards (Box 7B) are administered by external agents like supervisors. These rewards are the equivalent of Herzberg's hygiene factors and Maslow's lower order needs. They are usually reflected in factors like salary increases and promotions. The fact that the intrinsic rewards are directly related to personal performance is indicated by the solid connecting line in Exhibit 5.6.The criteria on which extrinsic rewards are distributed may not be related to performance. Thus, a wavy line has been used in Exhibit 5.6 between performance and extrinsic rewards. As an example, promotion could be based on seniority, not on performance. Likewise, salary increases could be fixed for every employee; relative performance may not be taken into account.

The receipt of rewards should lead to satisfaction (Box 9 in Exhibit 5.6). But, the relationship between receipt of rewards and satisfaction is dependent upon the individual's perception of whether the rewards were equitable (Box 8). Thus, the Porter and Lawler theory incorporates constructs from Adams' theory of inequity.

It should be pointed out that the relative performances of self and coworkers have a significant effect on how equity is perceived. Individuals who believe that they have performed well tend to emphasize performance as a standard for equity of rewards rather than the cost-benefit comparisons suggested by Adams' theory. An NBA player is not as concerned about the effort he put in to get to the NBA (or the effort put in during the season) as he is about recieving a salary comparable to other players whose *performance contributions* are similar. Thus, the importance of performance in the determination of equity of rewards is illustrated by the broken line between performance (Box 6) and perceived equitable rewards (Box 8). It should also be pointed out that the effect of perceived equity of rewards does not affect the relationship between intrinsic rewards and satisfaction because this relationship is internally experienced.

Finally, Exhibit 5.6. shows two feedback loops — one leading from satisfaction back to value of rewards, and the other leading from the relationship between performance and rewards back to perceived effort-reward probability. The first feedback reflects the fact that the receipt of rewards affects the values attached to those rewards. In the case of an extrinsic reward like pay, the value attached by employees to these rewards are likely to be lowered as more and more of it is received. Thus, an athlete who receives a high salary is less likely to emphasize salary increases as much as one on the low end of the pay scale. This view is also consistent with both the Maslow and Herzberg theories. They suggested that the lower order needs, once satisfied, cease to be motivators. However, Porter and Lawler acknowledged that the satisfaction derived from the intrinsic rewards is likely to lead the individual to value them more.

The second loop relates to the employee's perception of the probability that his/her efforts will result in the rewards sought. If a baseball organization habitually promotes its managers on the basis of seniority, the perceived relationships between effort-performance-promotion will be weakened. That is, an individual desiring promotion might not be triggered to work hard, since his/her perception would be that the best way to get a promotion would be to get old. Thus, as Porter and Lawler pointed out, the organizational practices have a great influence in determining the perceived connection between performance and rewards.

In overview, the Porter and Lawler model of work motivation is comprehensive enough to include the concepts of Maslow's Need Hierarchy Theory, Herzberg's Two-Factor Theory, Vroom's Expectancy Theory, and Adams' Theory of Inequity.

Motivation in Sport Organizations

The practical implication of the need theories, particularly, Herzberg's motivation-hygiene theory, is that the job must be designed in such a way that it triggers as well as satisfies the higher order needs of the worker. Hackman and Oldham's "job characteristics model" of motivation is also based on the notion that the motivating potential of jobs is a function of their characteristics — skill variety, task identity, task significance, autonomy, and feedback.

The principles behind "job enrichment", however, are contrary to the bureaucratic prescriptions. For instance, on the one hand, the principle of job enrichment leads to the suggestion that a person must be given "a complete natural unit of work". On the other hand, the bureaucratic concept of "division of labor" contributes to the suggestion that the job should be broken down into smaller units. Similarly, removing controls over employees and giving them additional authority (techniques of enriching a job) are contrary to the bureaucratic principles of division of work and hierarchy of authority respectively.

It was pointed out previously that concerns for rationality and efficiency, and for uniformity and consistency in organizational activities are the basis for the bureaucratic way of structuring jobs. On the other hand, individual needs are the basis for the practice of promoting job enrichment. These two apparently contradictory approaches to the design of jobs can be reconciled if individual differences in needs and their strengths are taken into account. This view was highlighted by Hackman and Oldham who stated that the motivational impact of the characteristics of the job is moderated by individual differences in the strength of growth needs (see Exhibit 5.4). Thus, individuals with a strong desire for achievement, responsibility, and recognition can be given enriched jobs while those who are low on those needs can be assigned to fractionated and routine jobs.

Further, organizations also differ in their purposes and processes, and in their environmental conditions. Such differences would also facilitate the matching of jobs, individuals, and organizational characteristics.

The categorization of sport organizations into professional service organizations and consumer service organizations (see Chapter 2) provides a basis for recommendations relating to the match up of jobs, individuals, and organizational characteristics. It was pointed out that professional service and consumer service organizations differ in the type of services they provide. Professional services are non-standardized in the sense that they are individualized to suit the needs of customers and their unique problems. Thus, a professional employee is required to use personal expertise and knowledge to solve the problem. If additional help from professional colleagues or associations are needed, it is still the employee's prerogative to seek that help. That is, the professional employee has almost complete autonomy and control. In addition, a job in a professional service organization has greater task significance attached to it than a job in a consumer service organization. Further, it possesses greater variety and variability, and involves whole units of work. From this perspective, jobs in professional service organizations are "enriched". This notion was emphasized by Mills, Hall, Leidecker, and Margulies (1983) when they proposed the "flexiform" model for the organization of a professional service organization (see Chapter 4).

The services in a consumer service organization are usually standardized in the sense that they involve minimal information processing by employees, and they are governed by rules and procedures to a much greater extent than is the case in professional service organizations (see Chapter 4). Thus, the employees in consumer service organizations do not experience autonomy and responsibility to the same extent as employees of professional service organizations. Further, their jobs are also lower on task significance, variety, and variability. Finally, their jobs tend to be more fractionated and routine in nature.

The above discussion does contribute to a conclusion that there is a great potential for enriching the jobs in consumer service organizations. But, is this feasible or practical? This question must be answered from two perspectives —the perspective of the employee and the perspective of the organization.

If the perspective of the employee is considered, it is obvious that an attempt must be made to match the person and the job. That is, job enrichment is meaningful only to the extent that the employee's growth need strength warrants such enrichment, and to the extent that the employee is capable of handling an enriched job. In the absence of either or both of these conditions, job enrichment would not have the desired effect of motivating the individual. In fact, it could be damaging to the individual's self-esteem if he/she failed to deal with the enriched job because of a lack of expertise and ability.

If the organizational perspective is considered, job enrichment is still feasible in a consumer service organization provided that the organization is relatively small with few employees. In the initial stages of growth, it would be possible, and, indeed, desirable to permit employees with autonomy and freedom to be individualistic in providing services to customers. But, as the organization grows and expands, there is an increase in services to a large number of customers. Then, the need for standardization increases, and, with it, the necessity to institute rules and procedures for the guidance of employees. Given a choice between cost-effectiveness and job enrichment, a profit oriented consumer service organization would prefer cost-effectiveness. An organization responsible for the management of a professional sport arena must have a standard protocol for its ticket sellers. That protocol may be monotonous and boring but it also would be cost-effective.

The resolution of the dilemma concerning whether to emphasize uniformity and consistency or a job enrichment protocol lies in the staffing procedures. Managers of consumer service organizations must determine the extent to which they can afford job enrichment, and then attempt to recruit those individuals whose needs and abilities match the characteristics of the target jobs that they offer.

Even in situations where it is feasible and practical to redesign a job for enrichment purposes, a manager may not have the authority to do so. For example, a middle line manager in a large organization may not be permitted to alter a job description that was drawn up by superiors. This problem is more acute in those organizations which are bureaucratically organized. A supervisor of ticket sellers (to use the previous example), may not have the independence to alter the protocol set out by the director of operations. This does not, however, preclude the manager from exercising a leadership function by intervening in the motivational process. This issue is discussed in the next chapter.

Volunteer organizations. The notion of matching individual needs to the job is more pertinent to volunteers in organizations. That is, those who join an organization as employees might be prepared to accept a job and its requirements for economic reasons; the satisfaction of other needs might be relatively less important. Volunteers, by definition, do not seek economic benefits through their membership in an organization. A volunteer might join an organization for several reasons — learning and growing, helping others, cultivating friendships, using present skills and learning new skills, gaining work experience, repaying a debt to society, and using leisure time more effectively.

While it is true that the volunteer organization and the services it provides might be innately attractive to volunteers, their continued membership and commitment to the organization is largely dependent upon the type of work assignment they receive as well as the satisfaction they derive from it. For example, when a community association requests assistance to organize a basketball league, to handle registration and organize a schedule, and to coach the teams, several members of the community might volunteer. The total organizational effort must be broken down into specific units of work. In turn, this work must be assigned to the volunteers. Some of the units (e.g., coaching a team) are high on autonomy, responsibility, significance, variety, and so on. Others (e.g., answering the telephone during registration) are simple and routine. There is a greater likelihood that the coaches will find their work more rewarding than the registration agents.

From a different perspective, some volunteers are high on the need for growth and power. They desire more complex and challenging tasks like coaching a team. Others prefer to handle the simpler and more routinized tasks. The proper matching of these individuals with the right type of work is the task of the manager. When there is a good fit between the task demands and the personal needs of the volunteers, the volunteers feel satisfied, and are more likely to continue to participate. When, there is a mismatch, however, the experience is frustrating for the volunteers. Individuals who have a high need for growth find the simple tasks meaningless and nonfulfilling. Conversely, individuals who are low on the growth need find the complex jobs frustrating and stressful. In order to decrease the likelihood that a mismatch will occur, managers of volunteer organizations should draw up job descriptions for all the activities to be carried out. Then, the volunteers can choose the activity they prefer.

In overview, the need based or content theories contribute to the suggestion that jobs must be enriched so that workers find them challenging and satisfying - so that they can fulfill higher order needs. But, job enrichment is not practical in certain kinds of organizations (e.g., a profit oriented consumer service organization). Further, any attempt to redesign jobs must take into account the needs and desires of the members. It is unreasonable to assume that all employees actively seek the satisfaction of higher order needs in the work place. This notion of person-task fit is most applicable to volunteer organizations.

Summary

The motivational basis of the leading function was emphasized through a discussion of relevant "content" theories of motivation (Maslow's Need Hierarchy Theory, Alderfer's ERG Theory, and Herzberg's Two-Factor Theory), and 'process" theories (Vroom's Expectancy Theory, Adams' Theory of Inequity, and Porter and Lawler's Model of Motivation). Further, the motivating potential of the work was described from the perspective of Hackman and Oldham's Job Characteristics Model. Finally, the relevance of "job enrichment" to sport organizations was discussed.

Questions for Discussion

1. From your experience as a student or an athlete, recall a situation in which you felt the happiest (or most satisfied). Narrate the sequence of events that led to this high feeling. How long did this feeling last? How did it affect your subsequent work, interpersonal relations, and your well-being? Similarly, recall an incident when you felt most unhappy (or most dissatisfied), and describe it along the same lines. Does your experience support Herzberg's Two-Factor theory? Explain.

2. Discuss the factors that contribute to perceptions of inequity among students.

3. Do tasks (in one sport or across different sports) differ in terms of the task characteristics outlined by Hackman and Oldham? What are the motivational implications of such differences?

References

Adams, J.S. (1963). Toward an understanding of inequity. *Journal of Abnormal Social Psychology, 67,* 422-436.

Adams, J.S. (1977). Inequity in social exchange. In: B.M. Staw (Ed.), *Psychological foundations of organizational behavior.* Santa Monica, Ca.: Goodyear Publishing Company.

Alderfer, C.P. (1972). *Existence, relatedness, and growth: Human needs in organizational settings.* New York: Free Press.

Alderman, R.B. (1974).*Psychological behavior in sport.* Philadelphia: W. B. Saunders Company.

Dunnette, M.D., Campbell, J.P., & Hakel, M.D. (1967). Factors contributing to job satisfaction and job dissatisfaction in six occupational groups. *Organizational Behavior and Human Performance, 2,* 143-174.

Hackman, J.R. (1969). Toward understanding the role of tasks in behavioral research. *Acta Psychologica, 31,* 97-128.

Hackman, J.R., & Oldham, G.R. (1976). Motivation through the design of work: Test of a theory. *Organizational Behavior and Human Performance, 16,* 250-279.

Hackman, J.R., & Oldham, G.R. (1980). *Work design.* Reading, Mass.: Addison-Wesley Publishing Company.

Herzberg, F. (1968). One more time: How do you motivate people? *Harvard Business Review,* January-February, 53-62.

Herzberg, F., Mausner, B., & Snyderman, B.B. (1959). *The motivation to work.* New York: John Wiley & Sons.

Hoy, W.K., & Miskel, C.G. (1982). *Educational administration: Theory, research, and practice.* New York: Random House.

Hulin, C.L. & Smith, P.A. (1967). An empirical investigation of two implications of the two-factor theory of job satisfaction. *Journal of Applied Psychology, 51,* 396-402.

Maslow, A.H. A theory of human motivation. *Psychological Review, 50,* 370-396.

Mills, P.K., Hall, J.L. Leidecker, J.K. & Margulies, N. (1983). Flexiform: A model for professional service organizations. *Acedemy of Management Review, 8,* 118-131.

Porter, L.W., & Lawler, E.E. (1968). *Managerial attitudes and performance,* Homewood, Ill.: Richard D. Irwin, Inc.

Rees, C.R. (1980). Motivation-hygiene theory and sport participation: Finding room for the 'I' in "Team". *Motor Skills: Theory into Practice, 4,* 24-31.

Scott, W.E. (1966). Activation theory and task design. *Organizational Behavior and Human Performance, 1,* 3-30.

Steers, R.M. (1975). Task-goal attributes, n Achievement, and supervisory performance. *Organizational Behavior and Human Performance, 13,* 392-403.

Steers, R.M. (1975). Effects of need for achievement on the job performance-job attitude relationship. *Journal of Applied Psychology, 60,* 678-682.

Turner, A.N., & Lawrence, P.R. (1965). *Industrial jobs and the worker.* Boston: Harvard University Press.

Vroom, V.H. (1964). *Work and motivation.* New York: John Wiley and Sons, Inc.

CHAPTER 6

LEADING: INTERPERSONAL PROCESSES

DEFINITION OF LEADERSHIP

THE TRAIT APPROACH

THE BEHAVIORAL APPROACHES

Ohio State Studies
Michigan Studies
Leader Behavior in Coaching

THE SITUATIONAL THEORIES OF LEADERSHIP

The Contingency Model of Leadership Effectiveness
Need for Power and Managerial Motivation
The Path-Goal Theory of Leader Effectiveness
Substitutes for Leadership
The Adaptive-Reactive Theory
The Multidimensional Model of Leadership

LEADERSHIP AND DECISION MAKING

SUMMARY

QUESTIONS FOR DISCUSSION

REFERENCES

The concept of leadership can be viewed from two perspectives. In the etymological sense, a leader is a person who actually leads the group. Thus, in early military history, a captain would lead the charge or attack while the brigade would follow. In other contexts, individuals such as Gandhi or Luther, based on personal convictions, would initiate some action. Others would follow in their footsteps either because they were convinced of the causes espoused by these leaders or because they were attracted by their personal qualities. But, the essence of this type of leadership, which is known as *charismatic leadership* (House, 1977), is that the leaders initiated and spearheaded a movement or activity.

From an organizational perspective, however, leadership is just one of the functions of a manager who is placed in charge of a group and its activities, and is, in turn, guided by superiors and organizational factors. The process of such leadership in this context does not require the leader to be out in front and/or working alongside the members. Further, the members need not have necessarily chosen this particular person to be their leader. It is the organization which has decided upon the members and their leader. This form of *organizational leadership* is the focus in the sections which follow.

The distinction between the two perspectives of leadership does not preclude the possibility that both types of leaders could be present in an organization. For example, the coach of an athletic team is a leader in the organizational sense. But, the team could also have a charismatic leader. Such famous athletes as Larry Bird in basketball and Wayne Gretzky in hockey are known to have inspired their teammates toward greater effort and performance. In management literature, leaders of this type are designated as *informal* leaders; the officially appointed managers are called the *formal* leaders. While both types of leaders do affect the members and their activities, the emphasis in this book is on the formal leaders and their influence on the group and its performance.

Definition of Leadership

The specification of goals, the identification of the courses of action to achieve those goals, the assignment of individuals and positions to carry out the specific activities, and the appointment of managers to coordinatethose activities are completed during the processes of planning and organizing. When these functions have been completed, it becomes the manager's responsibility to ensure that members carry out their assigned responsibilities. This function is leadership.

Most modern definitions of leadership refer to "the behavioral process of influencing individuals or groups toward set goals" (Barrow,1977, p. 232). That is, the notion of influencing others is a significant component of leadership. In fact, Hollander and Julian (1969) have suggested that the two terms — leadership and influence — are synonymous. Further, the process of influence is, in its very essence, interpersonal in nature. This requirement distinguishes the leading function from the other functions of a manager.In other words, while the planning, organizing, and evaluating functions can be largely carried out without significant interaction, the leading function requires interpersonal interaction between a manager and the members.

The definition presented above also specifies that leadership is a behavioral process, and, thus, emphasizes what the leader *does* rather than what the leader *is*. Although there is a general consensus on this issue, there has been continuous dialogue concerning whether what the leader does is a function of what the leader is, or whether doing and being are independent factors. This dialogue is reflected in the various theories of leadership. These theoretical approaches can be classified into three main categories: those that deal with the traits of leaders (the *trait approach*); those that deal with the behaviors of leaders (the *behavioral approach*); and, those that deal with the leader's traits and/or behaviors in a specific situational context — a context which takes into account the characteristics of both the members and the organization (the *situational approach*).

The Trait Approach

In early leadership research, an attempt was made to identify a finite set of personal characteristics that would distinguish good leaders. The personal characteristics studied included physical traits such as height, weight, age, and appearance; mental traits such as intelligence; personality traits such as aggressiveness, dominance, extroversion, self-esteem, achievement motive, and task orientation; social background characteristics such as education and socio-economic status; and, social or interpersonal skills. But, these research efforts did not yield any consistent findings — no universal set of traits were characteristic of effective leaders. This is one major reason why the general trait approach to the study of leadership fell into disfavor. Further, as Szilagyi and Wallace (1980) pointed out, this general trait approach was concerned with the *emergence* of leaders and not their *effectiveness*.

The Behavioral Approach

The futility of the trait approach led several researchers to focus on what a leader actually does to contribute to group performance and satisfaction. The most notable among these efforts were the major research programs undertaken at Ohio State University and the University of Michigan. The contributions made by these scholars are discussed below.

Ohio State Studies

A major thrust in the Ohio State studies was to identify and describe the leadership behaviors which are relevant to the organizational context. Toward this end, the Ohio State study identified a large number of leader activities and classified them into nine categories (Hemphill and Coons, 1957). Subsequently, however, it was concluded that it would be difficult to effectively use nine dimensions of leader behavior. Also, some of these nine dimensions were highly intercorrelated. Thus, the nine were collapsed to yield four dimensions of leader behavior (Halpin and Winer, 1957). Further research indicated that even these four behaviors could be condensed into two broad categories — *consideration* and *initiating structure* (Halpin and Winer, 1957).

Consideration is defined as leader behavior that reflects a leader's concern for members' well-being, and a concern for warm and friendly relations within the group. Initiating structure is defined as leader behavior that reflects a leader's concern for clarifying the roles for both the leader and the members, and a concern for effective performance on the group's tasks.

Three different scales were developed to measure the two dimensions of leader behavior. *The Leadership Behavior Description Questionnaire (LBDQ)* (Halpin and Winer, 1957) is a general measure which can be used in different organizational contexts. Fleishman's (1957a) *Supervisory Behavior Description Questionnaire (SBDQ)* was primarily developed for use in industrial contexts. And, finally, Fleishman (1957b) also developed the *Leadership Opinion Questionnaire (LOQ)* which is used to assess attitudes regarding leadership behaviors. In all three questionnaires, the same two dimensions of leader behavior - consideration and initiating structure — are measured. It is possible for a leader to be described as high on both dimensions, low on both, or high on one and low on the other. Thus, a leader's style can be located in one of the quadrants in Exhibit 6.1. Although there was a general expectation that leaders falling in Quadrant 2 — those that exhibit high levels of both consideration and initiating structure — would be most effective, research results did not support this position. This lack of support was mainly attributed to the fact that the Ohio scholars did not consider the situational elements that can interact with the behaviors of a leader to influence effectiveness.

Exhibit 6.1. Ohio State Leadership Styles.

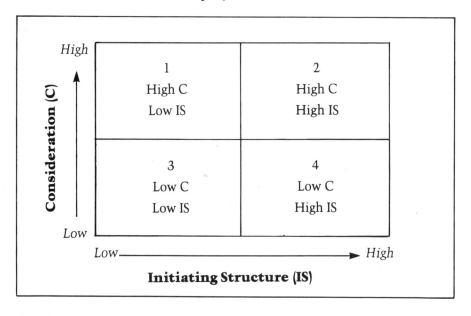

The Michigan Studies

The scholars at the University of Michigan were also concerned with the description of leader behaviors (Katz, Maccoby, and Morse, 1950; Katz, Maccoby, Gurrin, and Floor, 1951). In a manner identical to the Ohio State researchers, the Michigan group also identified two styles of leader behavior — an *employee orientation* or *employee-centered* leadership style, and a *production orientation* or *job-centered* leadership style. The employee orientation dimension reflects the degree to which a leader is concerned with the human relations aspect of the job. On the other hand, the production orientation dimension reflects the degree to which the leader is concerned with the technical aspects of the job and productivity.

Research carried out by the Michigan team showed that emphasis on either one of the dimensions resulted in increased productivity to almost the same extent. However, it was also observed that a production orientation caused a greater degree of employee resentment, dissatisfaction, turnover, and absenteeism (Morse and Reimer, 1956). It should be apparent that the

Michigan studies, which were carried out concurrently but independently of the Ohio State studies, yielded conceptually similar dimensions of leader behavior.

In 1966, Bowers and Seashore, in an effort to synthesize the results of earlier research involving both the Michigan and Ohio State descriptions of leader behavior, proposed a four-dimensional description of leader behavior. Their four dimensions included support, interaction facilitation, goal emphasis, and work facilitation. *Support* reflects behaviors that enhance a subordinate's feelings of personal worth and importance; *interaction facilitation* reflects behaviors which foster close and mutually satisfying relationships within the group; *goal emphasis* reflects behaviors which emphasize the group's goals and their attainment; and, *work facilitation* reflects behaviors that facilitate goal attainment by coordinating group activities and providing technical guidance. The scales to measure these four dimensions of leader behavior are contained in the *Survey of Organizations* (Taylor and Bowers, 1972).

In overview, these earlier research efforts were successful in identifying and describing relevant categories of leader behavior. But, they have been criticized for a number of reasons. One of these is that the complexity of leadership cannot be adequately described by two dimensions of leader behavior (House and Dessler, 1974; Stogdill, 1974; Yukl, 1981). (In fact, in Stogdill's (1974) extended version of the LBDQ, there are twelve dimensions of leader behavior. Similarly, Yukl's (1981) *Managerial Behavioral Survey (MBS)* consists of nineteen sub-scales.) But, questions relating to the appropriate number of leader behaviors are not as critical as the issue of the relationship between leader behavior and group performance. That is, it is immaterial how many dimensions are required to describe leader behavior if these dimensions do not show any relationship to the desired outcomes of group performance and member satisfaction.When viewed from this perspective, the earlier leadership studies have not been successful.

These earlier research efforts were also criticized because they have confounded the style of making a decision with the substance of the decision. For instance, in the LBDQ, the sub-scale which assesses initiating structure contains items which reflect the degree to which a leader possess a participative manner to make decisions. Similarly, the consideration subscale includes items that reflect the degree to which the leader possess a participative orientation. It has been argued (House and Dessler, 1974; House and Mitchell, 1974; Sheridan, Downey, and Slocum, 1975; Yukl, 1971; 1981). that the decision making aspects of leadership (autocratic versus participative versus delegative, and so on) should be viewed in isolation from other aspects (task oriented versus person oriented). In this regard, House and Mitchell (1974) have separated *participative behavior* (behavior which allows members to participate in decision making) from *instrumental behavior* (behavior which serves to control and coordinate activities), and *achievement-oriented behavior* (behavior which sets challenging goals and serves to express confidence in subordinates), from *supportive behavior* (which is behavior concerned with the welfare of the members and the creation of a pleasant work environment).

In Yukl's (1981) scale there is a dimension — *decision participation* — which measures "the extent to which a leader consults with subordinates and otherwise allows them to influence his or her decisions" (p. 122).

Finally, a third general criticism that has been levelled at the Ohio State and Michigan studies is that they do not assess the specific dimensions of leader behavior appropriate to specific contexts (House and Dessler, 1974; Sheridan, Downey, and Slocum, 1975; Yukl, 1971). That is, certain leader behaviors might be effective in certain situations, and ineffective in others. This issue is addressed by the situational theories of leadership which are discussed subsequently.

Leader Behavior in Coaching

There have been several attempts to study coaching behavior using the tests which incorporate the Ohio State dimensions of leader behavior. But, there have been very few attempts to define and describe the leader behaviors that are most relevant to coaching. One exception is the work of Chelladurai and Saleh (1980) and Chelladurai and Carron (1981). On the basis of their research with high school and university athletes from various sports, they identified five dimensions of leader behavior in sport situations — *training and instruction, social support, positive feedback, democratic behavior,* and *autocratic behavior.* These five dimensions are described in Exhibit 6.2. Two of the dimensions — training and instruction and positive feedback — are related to the process of task accomplishment and the degree of task accomplishment respectively. Social support is concerned with the social needs of members, individually and collectively. The final two dimensions —democratic behavior and autocratic behavior — are concerned with the degree to which the leader allows members to participate in decision making.

Situational Theories of Leadership

From a systems perspective of leadership, the situation consists of the leader, the members, and the organizational context in which they operate. The theories that view leadership from this perspective have generally tended to emphasize one of these elements more than the others. In the following sections, the theories that focus on the leader (Fiedler, 1967; McClelland and Burnham, 1976), those that focus on the members (House, 1971), and those that focus on the organization (Osborn and Hunt, 1975) are dealt with in order.

Exhibit 6.2. Dimensions of Leader Behavior in Sports.

Dimension	Description
Training and Instruction Behavior	Behavior of the coach aimed at improving the performance of the athletes by emphasizing and facilitating hard and strenuous training; by instructing them in the skills, techniques and tactics of the sport; by clarifying the relationship among the members; and by structuring and coordinating the activities of the members.
Democratic Behavior	Behavior of the coach which allows greater participation by the athletes in decisions pertaining to group goals, practice methods, and game tactics and strategies.
Autocratic Behavior	Behavior of the coach which involves independence in decision making and which stresses personal authority.
Social Support Behavior	Behavior of the coach characterized by a concern for individual athletes, for their welfare, for positive group atmosphere, and for warm interpersonal relations with members.
Rewarding (Positive Feedback) Behavior	Behavior of the coach which includes providing reinforcements for an athlete by recognizing and rewarding good performance.

Finally, the Multidimensional Model of Leadership (Chelladurai, 1978), which is a synthesis of the above theories, is discussed.

The Contingency Model of Leadership

The impetus toward situational approaches to leadership was first provided by Fiedler (1954, 1967, 1973). His *Contingency Model of Leadership Effectiveness* is based on the propositions that a leader's style (task orientation versus employee or interpersonal orientation) is a relatively stable personality characteristic; that the situation in which the leader operates may be more or less favorable to the leader (i.e., favorable to the leader in the exercise of influence over the subordinates); and, that leadership effectiveness is contingent upon the fit between the leader's style and the situational favorableness.

Leadership Style. As noted previously, leadership style refers to the tendency of an individual to emphasize task accomplishment (task orientation) or interpersonal relations (employee orientation) in a task situation. Fiedler introduced a unique method to assess leadership style. The respondent is asked to recall a *least preferred coworker* (LPC) — that is a person the respondent has had the greatest amount of difficulty working with in the past. Then, the respondent is asked to evaluate that least preferred coworker on a scale that consists of sixteen to twenty items (depending on the form used) which are bipolar adjectives. The following are three sample items from the scale:

Pleasant	__.__.__.__.__.__.__.__	Unpleasant
	8 7 6 5 4 3 2 1	
Tense	__.__.__.__.__.__.__.__	Relaxed
	1 2 3 4 5 6 7 8	
Efficient	__.__.__.__.__.__.__.__	Inefficient
	8 7 6 5 4 3 2 1	

An individual's score on this LPC Scale is considered to reflect the individual's leadership style. In Fiedler's (1967) view:

> we visualize the high-LPC individual (who perceives his least preferred coworker in a relatively favorable manner) as a person who derives his major satisfaction from successful interpersonal relationships, while the low-LPC person (who describes his LPC in very unfavorable terms) derives his major satisfaction from task performance. (p. 45)

Thus, the basic motivation of the high-LPC is primarily toward the development of warm and friendly interpersonal relations with subordinates while the basic motivation of the low-LPC is primarily toward task accomplishment. In a later revision of the theory, Fiedler (1972) suggested that the LPC score represents a two-level (primary and secondary) motivational system. That is, the primary orientation of the high-LPC is toward interpersonal relations. When that is achieved, the high-LPC leader focuses on task accomplishment (secondary motivation). On the other hand, the low-LPC focuses first on task accomplishment, and, when that goal is reached or is about to be reached, the focus may shift to fostering warm interpersonal relations.

Situational Favorableness. The favorableness of the situation reflects the degree to which the situation permits or facilitates the exercise of influence by the leader. According to Fiedler, there are three elements in the situation that affect its favorableness — *leader-member relations, task structure,* and *power position of the leader.*

Leader-member relations are a reference to the degree to which the members like and respect the leader. Thus, the more friendly the members are, the easier it is for the leader to exert influence. Fiedler viewed leader-member relations as the most important element contributing to the favorableness of the situation.

The second element in the situation affecting favorableness for the leader is the task itself. According to Fiedler, the more structured the task is, the more it contributes to situational favorableness. Task situations can vary in terms of *goal clarity* (the degree to which the requirements of the group are clearly defined), *goal-path multipilicity* (the degree to which a number and variety of procedures are required to accomplish the task), *decision verifiability* (the extent to which the outcomes of decisions can be easily evaluated), and *solution multiplicity* (the degree to which a number of correct solutions are possible). In the contingency model, the task of the group is considered to contribute to situational favorableness if the goals are clearly defined, if there are limited procedures to accomplish the task, if the output of the group can be easily measured, and, if there is only one possible standard to evaluate performance. In short, the more structured the group task is, the easier it is for the leader to influence the group.

The power position of the leader, the final element of situational favorableness, reflects the authority invested in the leader's position and the degree of control he/she has over rewards and sanctions. Thus, the greater the power of the leader, the greater the potential for influencing the members.

Fiedler's research showed that task oriented leaders (low-LPC) were more effective in situations very high or very low in favorableness. On the other hand, employee (relations) oriented leaders (high-LPC) were more effective in moderately favorable situations. These contingent relationships between leader's style and situational favorableness are illustrated in Exhibit 6.3. The Exhibit illustrates how situations can be placed along a favorableness continuum. At one end, the most favorable situations are found — the leader-member relations are good, task structure is high, and the leader power position is strong. At the other end, the most unfavorable situations are found — the leader-member relations are poor, the task is unstructured, and the leader power position is weak.

One implication of Fiedler's theory is that any leadership style can be effective provided it is matched with the situation and its favorableness.

148

Exhibit 6.3. Fiedler's Contingency Model of Leadership Effectiveness.

Reproduced with permission from P. Chelladurai and A.V. Carron, *Leadership*, Ottawa: Canadian
Association of Health, Physical Education and Recreation, 1978©, p. 25.

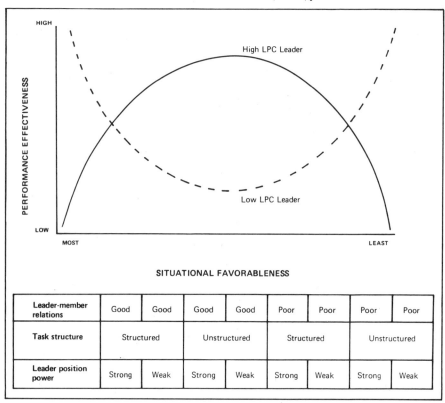

Another implication is that, since the leadership style is a stable personality characteristic, it is easier to change the situation than to change leadership style. Thus, an organization can change the composition of the group to alter the leader-member relations; or change the task structure by varying the extent of rules and procedures in the task situation; or increase the power (authority) of the leader. Also, the theory provides a practical guideline for aspiring managers/leaders. That is, the theory provides a basis for individuals to assess their own leadership style; evaluate the various positions of leadership open to them; and, then, choose the one position in which the situation's favorableness matches their personal leadership style.

Fiedler's contingency model has been extensively tested in different organizational contexts. It is not surprising that the research of Fiedler and his associates was supportive of the theory since the theory itself was built on that research. However, subsequent research by others has brought out some limitations of the theory. One issue pertains to the question of what the LPC Scale actually measures. Initially, it was viewed as a measure of personality, but a subsequent interpretation advanced by Fiedler (1973) was that it measures a hierarchy of goals (task accomplishment versus interpersonal relations). Larson and Rowland (1974) have suggested that the LPC measures the *cognitive complexity* of the individual (i.e., the extent to which an individual can process and assimilate numerous and complex bits of information).

Somewhat related to the above issue is the question of stability in a leader's orientation. Fiedler's model does not allow for the possibility of the shift in LPC scores due to experience with different groups. Further, in the model, task orientation and interpersonal orientation are treated as extremes on a single continuum. The possibility that a leader could be high on both orientations is not considered in the theory. Another limitation is that the theory overlooks the possibility that the managers's leadership style could actually change the situational characteristics. For example, a leader might be operating under the condition of poor leader-member relations. If that leader was a high-LPC (relations oriented), then his/her activities would tend to improve the leader-member relations, and, over time, the situation would become more favorable.

Another comment on the theory relates to the issue of task orientation (or relations orientation) versus the style of decision making. That is, according to the theory, a task oriented leader is autocratic in arriving at a decision and a relations oriented leader is democratic. As noted in the earlier discussion of the description of leader behavior, the assumption that a task (or relations) orientation is associated with a particular style of decision making is unjustified.

It is also questionable whether situations representing the extreme ends of the favorableness continuum (see Exhibit 6.3) are common in organizations. The least favorable situation on this continuum represents a chaotic situation that could not continue to exist for any length of time. Similarly, the most favorable situation on this continuum represents utopia.

Sport seems to be an area where the situation might be most favorable to the leader. Athletics are generally a voluntary activity. That is, individuals freely choose to participate. Quite often, athletes also have a choice of a team (and, consequently, the choice of a coach). Further, both the coach and the athletes share the organizational goal of pursuit of excellence. And, finally, the processes to achieve that goal are also clearly understood and accepted by all members of the organization. As a result, the three elements — the leader, the member, and the situation -are in congruence with each other. Consequently, the situation is very favorable for the exercise of influence by the coach — an autocratic coach could be very effective. In short, Fiedler's proposal that task oriented and autocratic leaders are most effective in highly favorable situations is reasonable in an athletic setting. In fact, a number of studies have found that coaches do tend to be generally autocratic and task oriented in their leadership style (e.g., Hendry, 1968, 1969; Ogilvie and Tutko, 1966).

In overview, despite the criticisms, Fiedler's contingency model was the first attempt to view leadership from a situational perspective. Fiedler emphasized the need to analyze the leadership style as well as the situational characteristics. Although the meaning of the LPC score is questionable, the theory has highlighted the significance of a leader's personality and orientations.

Need for Power and Managerial Motivation

While the needs for achievement, affiliation, and power are significant in influencing human behavior generally, they have specific relevance to the organizational context. This has been the focus of research by McClelland and his associates (McClelland, 1965, 1970, 1975; McClelland and Burnham, 1976; McClelland and Winter, 1969). The *need for achievement* refers to "the desire to do something better or more efficiently than it has been done before" (McClelleand and Burnham, 1976, p. 100). Individuals who have a high level of this need prefer a task that is moderately difficult rather than one which is too difficult or too easy. These same individuals also prefer rapid, specific feedback on how well they are doing. Further, since achievement-motivated people try to improve their personal performance, they tend to do things themselves.

These characteristics would benefit the owner/manager of an individual business and/or small firm. Thus, as Yukl (1981) pointed out, "the dominant motive for successful entrepreneurial managers appears to be need for achievement. Of course, success depends on the manager's ability as well as his motivation" (p. 79). When physical education graduates start businesses offering fitness services, they would have a greater chance of being successful if they were highly achievement oriented versus if they were low on that motive.

The perseverance, dedication, and work ethic which are characteristic of achievement-motivated people have led many theorists and practitioners to suggest that the need for achievement should be the dominant prerequisite for *all* successful managers. But, this is not necessarily the case in larger organizations where what the manager personally does is less important than what the subordinates do. As McClelland and Burnham (1976) suggested, "the manager's job seems to call more for someone who can influence people than for someone who does things better on his own. In motivational terms, then, we might expect the successful manager to have a greater 'need for power' than need to achieve" (p. 101).

Need for power refers to "a desire to have impact, to be strong and influential" (McClelland and Burnham, 1976, p. 103). For example, the success of deans of faculties of physical education is based on the degree to which they have influenced their faculty members towards greater effort and achievement rather than on what they have personally accomplished. A dean's willingness and ability to influence faculty members is far more critical than personal achievements. In contrast, it was already noted that in the case of the "fitness" entrepreneur, the need for achievement is most important.

McClelland and Burnham (1976) observed that the need for power must be moderated by a concern for the organization and the subordinates:"above all, the good manager's power is not oriented toward personal aggrandizement but toward the institution which he or she serves ....This is the 'socialized' face of power as distinguished from the concern for personal power" (p. 103). Again, a contrast between a dean and an entrepreneur helps to clarify the distinction between "socialized power" and "personalized power". The successful dean must exhibit controlled and socialized power. Since personal goals and organizational interests coincide in the case of the entrepreneur and since there are few others, if any, involved in the operation of the firm, the personalized power motive may not be detrimental to the success of the firm.

McClelland's emphasis on the power motive appears to be in opposition to a conventional "people orientation" and to the traditional reluctance to utilize an authoritarian form of management.McClelland and Burnham, however, have argued that:

> the bogeyman of authoritarianism has in fact been wrongly used to downplay the importance of power in management. After all, management is an influence game. Some proponents of democratic management seem to have forgotten this fact, urging managers to be primarily concerned with people's human needs rather than with helping them to get things done.(pp.104-105)

They noted that the presence of a power motive in management does not preclude the possibility that the manager could also adopt a democratic style. In fact, their research showed that successful managers were those who possessed a high need for power, a high concern for the organization, and who used a democratic managerial style. Subordinates under these types of managers possessed a high sense of responsibility and perceived a high degree of organizational clarity and team spirit (McClelland and Burnham, 1976).

The need for affiliation refers to the desire to be liked and be accepted by the group. According to McClelland and Burnham, the affiliation motive is least important to successful management. In fact, it has been suggested that it could even be detrimental to successful management. Managers with a high need for affiliation might tend to compromise on various rules in order to satisfy individual needs. While the individual recipients would enjoy this preferential treatment, other members of the organization would consider these practices as unfair. Thus, the morale of the group would be lowered. McClelland and Burnham concluded that

Oddly enough, the good manager in a large company does not have a high need for achievement ... although there must be plenty of that motive somewhere in his organization. The top managers ...have a high need for power and an interest in influencing others, both greater than their interest in being liked by people. The manager's concern for powers should be socialized — controlled so that the institution as a whole, not only the individual, benefits. (p. 109)

It must be noted that the above conclusion pertains to managers of large organizations. As noted before, in the case of small firms and entrepreneurs, the achievement motive and/or personalized power motive might not adversely affect managerial effectiveness.

In overview, the two approaches described above — Fiedler's contingency model of leadership effectiveness and McClelland's view of managerial motivation — emphasize the importance of specific personal traits of the leader. Although Fiedler's task orientation and McClelland's power motivation appear to be similar to the extent that both focus on task accomplishment, there is one significant difference between them. While Fiedler's task-oriented leader is autocratic (by definition), McClelland's power-motivated managers could also express their power motive in democratic ways. This difference notwithstanding, both Fiedler and McClelland have highlighted the significance of personal traits for effective leadership.

The Path-Goal Theory of Leader Effectiveness

In contrast to the theories described earlier, the Path-Goal Theory of leader effectiveness focuses on members and their personal attributes. The theory was first proposed by Evans (1970) and later expanded upon by House and his associates (House, 1971; House and Dessler, 1974; House and Mitchell, 1974). The essence of the theory was succinctly outlined by House (1971):

the motivational function of the leader consists of increasing personal pay-offs to subordinates for work-goal attainment, and making the path to these pay-offs easier to travel by clarifying it, reducing road blocks and pitfalls, and increasing the opportunities for personal satisfaction en route. (p. 323)

Since the theory focuses on members' personal goals and their perceptions of the organizational goals, and the most effective paths to these goals, it is called the path-goal theory of leader effectiveness. That is, the theory attempts to specify how leadership should clarify the path(s) of members to desired goals/rewards.

As was noted in the discussion of the classification of leader behavior, four classes of leader behavior are taken into account in the path goal theory —*instrumental behavior, supportive behavior, participative behavior, and achievement-oriented behavior* (House and Mitchell, 1975). Instrumental behavior is similar to the traditional initiating structure dimension. It is leader behavior which serves to clarify for members what is expected. It also involves leader behaviors associated with planning and coordinating. Supportive behavior reflects the concern of the leader for the welfare of the members and for a warm and friendly environment in the work place. Thus, this dimension is very similar to the consideration dimension from the Ohio State studies. Participative behavior reflects the degree to which a leader shares information with members and allows for participation in decision-making. Finally, achievement-oriented behavior reflects the degree to which challenging goals are set, good performance is expected, and confidence is expressed in the members.

The path-goal theory is composed of two basic propositions. The first is that the leader's function is a supplemental one. That is, a leader's behavior will have an impact on member motivation and effort only to the extent that such behavior is seen as an immediate source of rewards and satisfaction, or as instrumental to future rewards and satisfaction. Also, the leader's function supplements other factors that might contribute to member motivation, and those that might be supportive of the individual. In other words, leadership is most necessary when there is a lack of motivation in the organizational context in which the members operate.

The second proposition of the path-goal theory is that the motivational effect of leadership is a function of the situation which, in turn, is comprised of the members and the environmental pressures and demands. According to the theory, the personality and perceived ability of members affect the degree to which they prefer and/or react to specific forms of leader behavior. For instance, subordinates with a high need for affiliation would prefer supportive leadership behaviors while subordinates with a high need for achievement would prefer achievement-oriented leadership behaviors (House and Dessler, 1974). Similarly, a member who has a high perception of personal ability would prefer less instrumental leadership behavior (and in fact, would react negatively to such behavior).

The environmental pressures and demands are reflected by the nature of the task, organizational factors, and the primary work group. Tasks may vary in the degree to which they are routine or variable; to the extent to which they are interdependent; and to the degree to which they are inherently satisfying. In so far as the leader's role is supplemental, the leader's behavior should vary according to the demands of the task. Thus, instrumental behavior is more appropriate when the task is a variable one than when it is a routine one.

Similarly, interdependent tasks require a greater degree of coordination than independent tasks, and, therefore, a leader's instrumental behavior is appreciated more in the former case than in the latter case. These propositions were supported by Chelladurai and Carron (1982). They found that athletes in interdependent sports (team sports), and athletes in variable sports (such as basketball) preferred more training and instruction (i.e., instrumental behavior) than athletes in independent sports and nonvariable sports (such as track and field). In short, the degree to which a leader's behavior will be acceptable to the members, and the degree to which that behavior will have a motivational impact is dependent on the nature of the task.

The nature of the work group also influences the degree to which specific leader behaviors are necessary and relevant. For example, in a closely knit work group, the necessary guidance and coaching may be provided by the senior members of the group. In such a case, a leader's instrumental behavior is redundant. Similarly, supportive behaviors are unnecessary since the cohesive group would fulfill that need.

The final element in the situation is the organizational set. That is, the goals of the organization, the rules and procedures laid down, and other organizational practices serve to determine the need for and the effects of leader behavior. Thus, when an organization has extensive rules and procedures for each member concerning how to carry out assigned tasks, the leader's instrumental behavior becomes unnecessary.

The path-goal theory of leadership can be better understood if it is viewed from the perspective of individual motivation. To facilitate such a perspective, Chelladurai (1981) presented a modified version of the Porter and Lawler model of motivation (see Chapter 5) and discussed the relevance of the various dimensions of coaching behavior (see Exhibit 6.4) to the motivational process.

As Exhibit 6.4 shows, motivation is considered to be a function of both the values attached to the rewards and probability estimates that effort will lead to the rewards. The effort-performance relationship (Box 2 to Box 3) is moderated by the members ability (Box 6) and the accuracy of the perception of his/her role (Box 7). Finally, the reward-satisfaction relationship (Box 4 to Box 5) is influenced by member's perception of the equity of the rewards (Box 8).

Based on this framework of individual motivation, it is possible to identify the points along the motivation - performance - satisfaction sequence where the leader should intervene in an attempt to enhance the motivational state of the individual. First, the value an individual attaches to intrinsic rewards is heightened when the leader sets challenging goals and expresses confidence in the member's capacity to attain those goals (achievement-oriented behavior). Supportive behavior (Box A) makes the effort phase enjoyable and frees it from any interpersonal frictions. Instrumental leader behavior (Box B) is beneficial

Exhibit 6.4. Leader Behavior and Individual Motivation.

Modified from Chelladurai (1981).

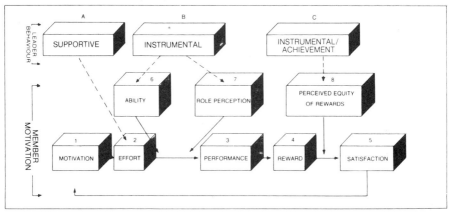

when it leads to the development of the member's ability and when it serves to clarify role expectations. Thus, instrumental behavior strengthens the relationship between effort and performance. Participative behavior also contributes to a member's role clarity as well as to feelings of involvement in such decisions. Both of these effects of participative behavior enhance role performance. Finally, the equitable distribution of a leader's personal rewards (i.e., equal rewards for equal performance) leads to a sense of equitability among the members.[1]

In overview, although the path-goal theory of leadership includes a number of situational parameters, the greatest emphasis is placed on the members, their ability, and their personal dispositions.[2] Leadership is viewed as a process by which members are helped in the attainment of their personal goals (in so far as they are aligned with organizational goals). In contrast to Fiedler's contingency model, the path-goal theory contains the implicit assumption that a leader can change his/her leadership style according to situational exigencies.

1. The emphasis on *personal rewards* is deliberate. In small organizations, the manager may have considerable control over the rewards offered by the organization. In contrast, in larger organizations, the manager may not have a great deal of input into the determination of individual rewards. For example, pay raises and/or promotions in a bureaucracy are a function of some preset requirements and/or seniority. Under these circumstances, the manager must be content with providing personal rewards like praise and encouragement.

2. Hersey and Blanchard (1969, 1977) based their Situational Theory of Leadership on the concept of *maturity* of members, which was defined as "the capacity to set high but attainable goals (achievement motivation), willingness and ability to take responsibility, and education and/or experience of an individual or group" (Hersey and Blanchard, 1977, p. 161). Thus, their theory combines ability and personality into one construct — maturity. According to the situational theory, a leader should reduce task behavior (i.e., structuring behavior) and increase relationship behavior (i.e., consideration) as members progress from low maturity to moderate levels of maturity. Beyond the moderate level of maturity, a leader should reduce both task and relationship behaviors. In sum, the situational theory is conceptually similar to the path-gold theory. The difference lie in the operationalisation of the concepts involved.

Substitutes for Leadership

It was pointed out that one of the propositions of the path-goal theory is that the leader's function is only supplemental. That is, the leader is expected to provide guidance and coaching, to structure activities for the members, and to provide social support only to the extent that these are lacking in the work environment. What this means is that whatever function the leader must perform may be partially accounted for by other factors in the environment. Kerr and Jermier (1978) have listed a number of such factors which they referred to as *substitutes for leadership*. The most significant ones are the members' characteristics, their professional orientation and affiliation, the nature of their task and the work group, and the organizational structure (including the policies and procedures).

The significance of member characteristics and the nature of the task was discussed earlier. The work group (or peer group) can also serve as a substitute for the leader. For example, a new student at a college or university receives assistance during the orientation period from classmates. Similarly, in work situations, fellow employees provide the guidance and coaching necessary to carry out assignments. More importantly, the work group also provides the social support necessary when both personal and organizational problems arise.

If the organizational policies and procedures are elaborate and if they clearly specify what the employee should do, and how, and under what circumstances (as is the case in bureaucracies), then the leader's instrumental behavior becomes redundant. The employee simply has to follow the rules. It was noted in Chapter 2, that within consumer service organizations, the concern for the standardization of services results in a tendency to fractionate jobs, and to specify extensive rules. Thus, a leader's instrumental behavior tends to be redundant. However, since consumer service tasks are relatively routine and monotonous, the leader must attempt to create a warm climate, and establish good interpersonal relationships within the group. Thus, the leader's supportive behavior is important.

In professional service organizations, the professional orientation of the members and their relationship with other professionals serve as substitutes for leadership. Professional orientation ensures that members are committed to providing a quality service. Further, professional associations set standards of performance for their profession, and these standards, in turn, are internalized by the members. In addition, periodic meetings of peers, and professional publications also provide some guidance and incentives for greater productivity. Given this orientation within professional service organizations, it becomes unnecessary for the leader to attempt to influence the members.

In cases, where there are numerous substitutes for leadership, a manager's attempts to influence members must be minimal; otherwise, there is the risk that the leadership will be viewed as interference.

The Adaptive-Reactive Theory.

Although both Fiedler and House included organizational variables among the elements in their respective theories, their treatment of them was superficial. Osborn and Hunt (1975) noted that the variables of the larger organizational system have an impact on both the leader and members, and, therefore, must be treated as separate classes of contingency variables. One class of variables in the organizational system, which are called *macro variables*, includes unit size, level of technology, and formal structure of the organization. A second class of contingency variables, which are called *micro variables*, includes the task itself and differences among individual members. On the basis of these two classes of variables which influence a leader, Osborn and Hunt dichotomized leader behavior into *adaptive behavior* and *reactive behavior*.

Adaptive behavior refers to the degree to which the leader adapts to the requirements of the organizational system. That is, the nature of the organization and its processes do demand and/or constrain leader behavior in specific ways. A football team and a badminton team provide a good example from sport. First, the football team is larger than the badminton team (unit size). Therefore, the control exerted and the guidance provided are necessarily different for a coach of a badminton team with 4 players versus the coach of a football team with 40 players. Secondly, football consists of highly differentiated and specialized positions while badminton does not. Thus, unit size and level of technology contribute to a need for different formal structures (a large coaching staff in football, hierarchical in nature with differentiated responsibilities). These, in turn, contribute to the emergence of different leader behaviors.

The micro variables in the Osborn and Hunt theory — the nature of the task and individual differences — are the same as those in the path-goal theory. The contrast between football and badminton again serves to illustrate the significance of the nature of the task. While the individual tasks in football involve relatively more large muscle groups, badminton tasks involve relatively finer movements. Also, while football is an interdependent sport, badminton is an independent sport. These differences, in turn, influence leader behavior. For example, talking loudly or shouting by a football coach might positively affect the players and the team. But, such behaviors would be detrimental to the performance of the badminton players. It was already noted that individual differences relating to personality and ability also influence leader behavior. The leader behaviors influenced by the task and individual differences are called the reactive behaviors — they reflect a leader's reactions to the needs and desires of the members.

Thus, according to the adaptive-reactive theory, the organizational variables (macro variables) control and constrain one set of leader behaviors (adaptive behaviors). Also, they do not permit the leader to deviate significantly from the organizational requirements. On the other hand, the micro variables elicit reactive behaviors which are largely under the control of the leader. The most important postulate of the adaptive-reactive theory is that the reactive behaviors reflect the discretionary influence exercised by the leader. Consequently, they will be motivational to the extent that they match the needs and preferences of the members.

The Multidimensional Model of Leadership

In the theories presented to this point, leadership is viewed from different perspectives but, in every instance, only a limited number of variables is considered to be relevant. For instance, in Fiedler's (1967) contingency theory, leadership style and the situational favorableness (described in terms of leader-member relations, task structure, and position power) are highlighted. However, the effects of member characteristics are ignored. On the other hand, in House's (1971) path-goal theory, members' needs and the task are taken into account but the characteristics of the leader are not considered. Similarly, in Osborn and Hunt's adaptive-reactive theory, the leader characteristics are not included.

From a systems point of view, there is a need to combine the various theoretical perspectives in order to gain an insight into the gestalt of leadership. The Multidimensional Model of Leadership (Chelladurai, 1978; Chelladurai and Carron, 1978) is an attempt to synthesize and to reconcile existing theories of leadership. A schematic illustration of the main components of the model is presented in Exhibit 6.5.

Essentially, the model focuses on the three primary types of leader behavior — *required, preferred,* and *actual.The antecedent variables that determine these leader behaviors are classified into situational characteristics, members characteristics,* and *leader characteristics.* The consequences (output or dependent variables) in the model are group *performance* and *satisfaction.*

Required Leader Behavior. As noted by Osborn and Hunt (1975), behaviors of a leader are to some extent dictated by the demands and constraints of the organization and its environment. The situational characteristics outlined by Osborn and Hunt —group size, its technology, and its formal structure — are included in the multidimensional model. In addition, the task of the group, the organizational goals, and the norms of a particular social setting are other situational characteristics that influence and control leader behavior.

Since the construct of leadership refers to a group, and since it is necessary to study leader behavior in terms of group's tasks, processes, and performance, the task of the group is considered a macro variable. This point is clarified by the fact that under one organizational setting — for example, a faculty of physical education — different units (or groups) may be involved in the performance of different tasks. In a physical education faculty, this could

Exhibit 6.5. A Multidimensional Model of Leadership.
Adapted from Chelladurai, 1978.

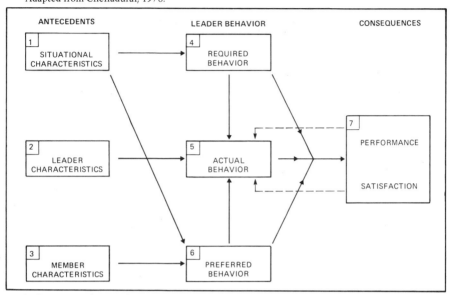

include the undergraduate, graduate, intercollegiate, and intramural programs. This same point also applies to the different athletic teams within a university. For each team and, of course, its coach, the group task becomes a part of the situation. Thus, the group task (as well as the other macro variables) imposes a common set of demands and constraints on all the group members.

In the multidimensional model, organizational goals are treated as a factor that affects the total group including the leader. For instance, the potential concern with quality versus quantity in a production firm affects both the manager's and the employee's behavior. In the athletic field, the professional athletic clubs have certain behavioral expectations for a coach that are different from those that are held by educational institutions for their coaches. These differing sets of expectations, in turn, have an influence on the behavior of the athletes involved.

Also included among the situational characteristics are the norms and codes of conduct prevalent (or emerging) in a given social setting. Contrast, for instance, the social norms surrounding a coach versus those surrounding a high school principal. The social norms of the athletic setting permit a coach to yell and scream at the players while such behaviors are proscribed in the case of a principal.

In summary, the situational variables (unit size, technology, formal structure, group task, organizational goals, and the norms and behavioral expectations in a particular social context) influence and control a portion of a leader's behavior. That portion of leader behavior controlled by the situational factors is referred to as the *required leader behavior*. These required behaviors tend to be task oriented and/or instrumental in the realization of the group's objectives (Osborn and Hunt, 1975).

Leader Behavior Preferred by Members. The preferences of members for specific leader behaviors stem from both the situational characteristics and the characteristics of the members. The impact of the task (and its characteristics of interdependence and variability) is an immediate determinant of member preferences (House, 1971; House and Dessler, 1974). The unit size, the technology, the goals, and the norms of the group also influence what members prefer from their leader.

Individual difference factors also influence members' preferences for particular leader behaviors. For example, the effect of task relevant ability is highlighted in the path-goal theory (House, 1971; House and Dessler, 1974). Similarly, a number of personality traits such as need for affiliation and need for achievement are also assumed in the path-goal theory to influence members' preferences for different leader behaviors. Lorsch and Morse (1974) and Morse (1976) suggested that an individual's attitude toward authority affects his/her reactions toward different types of supervision. Cognitive complexity refers to the way individuals process information. It is also expected to determine, in part, the preference for structuring behavior from the leader (Wynn and Hunsaker, 1975). Authoritarianism and the need for independence affect the degree to which members prefer their leader to use participation in decision making (Vroom, 1959). Those high in achievement motivation prefer the leader to provide challenge, responsibility, and feedback (McClelland, 1961). The interpersonal needs (e.g., need for affiliation, succorance, and so on) of members also affect their preferences for specific leader behaviors.

Actual Leader Behavior. The third, and obviously the most central, state of leader behavior is actual behavior. Two of the determinants of actual leader behavior are the macro variables and the preferences of members which were discussed earlier. Osborn and Hunt (1975) referred to the leader's adaptation to the dictates of the macro variables as adaptive behavior; the responses to the needs and desires of subordinates as reactive behavior. The extent to which leaders emphasize either adaptive behavior or reactive behavior or both is a function of their personal characteristics — particularly, personality and ability.

Any discussion of the leader's personality as a determinant of behavior must include Fiedler's (1967) global dichotomy of task oriented versus group oriented leader styles. Other personality traits of the leader that might affect actual leader behavior include authoritarianism, dogmatism, domination, cognitive complexity, need for achievement, need for affiliation, and need for power.

In the multidimensional model, the leader is assumed to be flexible and capable of altering his/her behavior according to changing conditions. This perspective is consistent with the position taken by Fiedler. He suggested that task oriented leaders would expand their focus once the task was accomplished and that the relations oriented leaders would emphasize the task after securing good relations with the members. The feedback loops in Exhibit 6.6 represent the processes through which such changes in leader behavior occur.

Ability of the leader is made up of two components. One of these is the leader's specific knowledge and expertise concerning various aspects of the group task and the processes necessary for the attainment of group's goals. This specific ability would vary with different leadership positions. In a government bureaucracy, knowledge of all the complex rules and regulations governing the activities of the group would represent this type of ability. Ability in this context is analogous to the technical skills introduced by Katz (see Chapter 1).

The second component of ability includes the leader's capacity to analyze the complexities of a problem (conceptual skill), and to persuade subordinates about the efficiency of a particular approach (human skill). This is a general ability which is transferable across situations.

Performance and Satisfaction. The consequences of the three types of leader behavior are performance and satisfaction. (Exhibit 6.6). An assumption of the multidimensional model is that the degree to which the three states of leader behavior are congruent, (actual behavior is in harmony with preferred behavior and required behavior) will influence performance and satisfaction. Any of the states of leader behavior could be a limiting factor.

For example, in some bureaucratic organizations, outdated and dysfunctional rules and regulations might be a requirement within the system and might be enforced by managers. But, these rules also might be intensely disliked by employees and, therefore, performance and satisfaction would be reduced. Similarly, if actual leader behavior deviated from the requirements of the organization and/or member preferences, it would detrimentally affect performance and satisfaction.

In overview, the multidimensional model takes into account the characteristics of the situation, the leader, and the members, and conceptualizes three states of leader behavior — required, preferred, and actual leader behaviors. The degree of congruence among these three states of leader behavior is assumed to be related to group performance and member satisfaction.

Leadership and Decision Making

In the previous sections, it was repeatedly emphasized that it is necessary to differentiate between the style of decision making (i.e., the degree to which the leader allows the members to participate in making decisions) and other forms of leader behaviors. The rationale for this viewpoint is that the degree to which members should be allowed to participate in decision making is a function of the situation in which the decision is made. In some situations, an authoritarian approach is essential, in others, a participative approach would be most effective, and, finally, in others, the decision should be delegated. Modern prescriptions for management emphasize, of course, the need for increased participation by members in decision making. These modern prescriptions are based on the assumption that a participative decision (1) results in increased rationality because more information is brought to the situation; (2) leads to greater acceptance by members; and, therefore, (3) leads to better implementation (Likert, 1967; Maier, 1974; McGregor, 1960). Further, from another perspective, the participative style of decision making is said to contribute to the self-esteem and growth of members (Likert, 1967; McGregor, 1960).

There are, however, some disadvantages associated with participative decision making which reduce its practicality and effectiveness. First, participative decisions take more time because members need time to discuss the various issues. Often, these discussions become tangential to the main issue, or relate to trivial issues. Second, the assumption that members can provide more information relating to the problem is not necessarily true. It is quite likely that the leader will have more information than all of the members combined. In this case, rationality is not enhanced. (In fact, a group discussion may be little more than the "pooling of ignorance".) Finally, participative decisions have the desired effects of enhancing group acceptance only if the members of the group are integrated. If the group is marked by internal rivalry and interpersonal conflicts, a participative style of decision making may serve as another disruptive force in the group.

Because no one single approach to decision making is effective in all situations, several models of participation have been proposed. Each includes a different set of contingency factors (e.g., Bass and Valenzi, 1974; Heller and Yukl, 1969; Maier, 1963; Tannenbaum and Schmidt, 1973; Vroom and Yetton, 1973). The model developed by Vroom and his associates (Vroom and Jago, 1978; Vroom and Yetton, 1973) is the most comprehensive, and has been subjected to empirical verification. Thus, it is discussed in this book.

Initially Vroom and his colleagues identified five procedures associated with the social processes of decision making. These vary in the degree of participation by members:

Autocratic I (AI) - the leader personally makes the decision based on the information available;

Autocratic II (AII) - the leader secures the necessary information from the members and, then, makes the decision personally.

Consultive I (CI) - the leader shares the problem with relevant members on an individual basis, takes their ideas into account, and, then, makes the decision alone.

Consultive II (CII) - the leader shares the problem with all the members as a group, takes their views into account, and, then, makes the decision alone.

Group II (GII) - the leader shares the problem with the group, lets the group generate and evaluate alternative solutions, and, then, arrives at a consensus solution. The role of the leader in this decision procedure is that of a chairperson.

It should be noted that only the last procedure (GII) is truly democratic —the members actually make the decision. In all the other situations, the leader is the sole decision maker. However, the degree to which the leader allows members to influence the decision increases from a purely autocratic procedure (AI) to consultation with the total group (CII).

The basic assumption within the Vroom model is that the appropriateness of each of these five decision processes for any given problem is dependent upon the attributes of that problem. After identifying eight attributes which are present in varying degrees in all decision-making situations, Vroom and Yetton presented their model in the form of a decision tree. This decision tree is illustrated in Exhibit 6.6. The eight problem attributes are listed as questions on the top of the decision tree. According to Vroom and Yetton, a leader can proceed along one or another branch of the tree (to a prescribed decision style) on the basis of his/her response to each of the questions (problem attributes). At the end of each of the branches a set of feasible decision styles are presented for the leader's use with that specific problem.

The first of the eight problem attributes included in the model is the requirement of *quality* in the decision. That is, is the problem significant enough to warrant a rational decision, or can a satisficing decision be made (see Chapter 3 for a discussion of maximizing and satisficing in decision making)?

The second attribute relates to the extent to which the *leader has information* regarding both the problem and the preferences of the members. Also, the amount of *information possessed by members* to make a quality decision is another attribute of the problem situation.

The extent to which the *problem is structured* is also a factor that influences the choice of a decision process. A problem is structured when only a minimal amount of readily available information is necessary, and when there are specific procedures to solve the problem. An unstructured problem requires the processing of complex and varied bits of information which are widely distributed among members.[3]

3. These first four attributes relate to the rationality of the decision process: they influence the quality of the decision. The final four attributes relate to the group's acceptance (or commitment to) the decision made.

164

Exhibit 6.6. The Vroom-Yetton Model of Decision-Making.

Reproduced with permission from V.H. Vroom and P.W. Yetton, *Leadership and Decision-Making*, Pittsburgh; University of Pittsburgh Press. 1973©, p. 194.

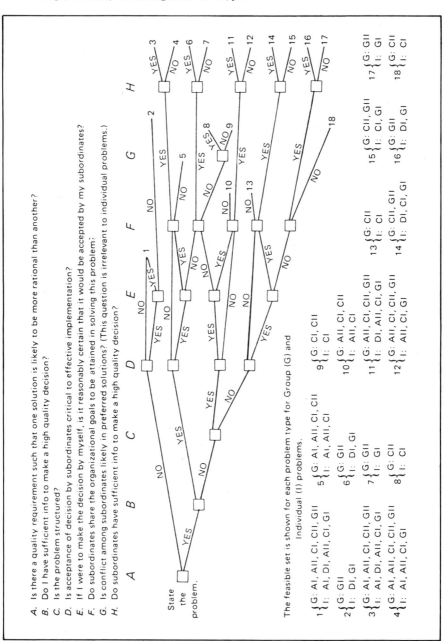

Group's acceptance or commitment is the fifth attribute that influences the choice of a decision process. Some problems falling outside the group's activities may not entail the involvement of the group. Further, in some cases, group compliance, not group commitment may be required.

Even when group acceptance is critical, the group may be already predisposed to accept a leader's autocratic decision. This *prior acceptance* could emanate from the perceived legitimacy of the leader's authority, from the leader's control over rewards and punishments, from the leader's expertise and knowledge, or from the affection that the members have for the leader (French and Raven, 1959).

The seventh attribute in the problem situation is the degree to which the *members are motivated* to attain the group's goals. As Vroom and Yetton (1973) pointed out "the quality of the decision is dependent not only on the information and expertise of those participating in it, but also on their disposition to use their information in the service of the goal stated in the problem" (p. 29).

Finally, the choice of a decision process is also affected by the likelihood of *conflict over preferred solutions*. These types of disagreements could arise because different members possess different bits of information or because they have differential perceptions of personal gains/losses.

The Vroom-Yetton model is usually illustrated in the form of the decision tree presented in Exhibit 6.6. The selection of a feasible set of decision styles is based on the application of specific rules which eliminate one or more of the decision processes for each problem type. For example, if the quality of the decision is important and the leader does not possess the necessary information and expertise, the AI style of making the decision is eliminated from the feasible set of alternatives. Similarly, when the quality of the decision is important and the members do not share the organizational goals, the GII process is eliminated from the feasible set of alternatives.

Vroom and Yetton (1973) suggested that when more than one decision process is feasible, the leader should select the one which requires the least amount of time. Thus, at terminal node #3 in Exhibit 6.6, all five decision processes are listed as feasible. According to Vroom and Yetton, the leader could reasonably use the AI style because it is clearly the quickest.

Research on the Vroom and Yetton model in management and industry has consistently shown that the situational attributes influence the manager's choice of a decision style approximately four times more often than individual difference (personal) factors. Also, in an athletic context, basketball players' preferences for a particular decision style were shown to be influenced by the problem attributes to a much greater extent than individual differences (Chelladurai and Arnott, 1985).

In overview, the Vroom-Yetton model is based on the proposition that situations can be characterized as autocratic or democratic, and that the specific characteristics of a problem determine the type of decision process that is most effective. It represents a logical and rational framework for managers to analyze problem situations and select an appropriate decision style.

In decision making, the manager must be concerned with both cognitive processes and social processes. The cognitive processes are associated with the generation and evaluation of alternatives — they contribute to the rationality of decisions. The social processes refer to the degree and type of involvement of the members in decision making.

Summary

Leadership defined as an influence process was described from different theoretical perspectives. The relative emphasis placed by the various theories on the leader, the members, and the organization was highlighted. These differing orientations constitute a multidimensional model of leadership. Finally, the relevance of the theories to sport organizations was discussed.

Questions for Discussion

1. Are you relatively more task oriented or relations oriented? What is the basis of your self-perception?

2. In the case of an athletic team, what factors serve as "substitutes for leadership"?

3. It has been suggested that sport is generally an autocratic situation. Do you agree or disagree with this position? Why?

4. Recall one of your work experiences (either part-time or full time). Describe the leadership provided by your supervisor in terms of one of the leadership theories discussed in the chapter.

References

Barrow, J.C. (1977).The variables of leadership: A review and conceptual framework. *Academy of Management Review*, 2, 231-251.

Bass, B.M., and Valenzi, E.R. (1974). Contingency aspects of effective management styles. In J.G. Hunt and L.L. Larson (Eds.), *Contingency approaches to leadership*. Carbondale,Ill.: Southern Illinois University Press.

Bowers, D.G., and Seashore, S.E. (1966). Predicting organizational effectiveness with a four-factor theory of leadership. *Administrative Science Quarterly*, 11, 238-263.

Chelladurai, P.(1978). *A contingency model of leadership in athletics*. Unpublished doctoral dissertation. University of Waterloo, Waterloo, Canada.

Chelladurai, P.(1981). The coach as motivator and chameleon of leadership styles. *Science Periodical on Research and Technology in Sport*. Ottawa: Coaching Association of Canada.

Chelladuari, P., and Arnott, M. (1985). Decision styles in coaching: Preferences of basketball players. *Research Quarterly for Exercise and Sport*, 56, 15-24

Chelladurai, P., and Carron, A.V. (1978). *Leadership*. Ottawa: Canadian Association for Health, Physical Education, and Recreation.

Chelladurai, P., and Carron, A.V. (1981). Applicability to youth sports of the Leadership Scale for Sports. *Perceptual and Motor Skills*, 53, 361-362.

Chelladurai, P. and Carron, A.V. (1982). Task characteristics and individual differences and their relationship to preferred leadership in sports. *Psychology of motor behavior and sport - 1982: Abstracts*. Maryland: North American Society for the Psychology of Sport and Physical Activity.

Chelladurai, P., and Saleh, S.D. (1980). Dimensions of leader behavior in sports: Development of a leadership scale. *Journal of Sport Psychology*, 2, 34-45.

Evans, M.G. (1970). The effects of supervisory behavior on the path-goal relationships. *Organizational Behavior and Human Performance*, 5, 277-298.

Fiedler, F.E. (1954). Assumed similarity measures as predictors of team effectiveness. *Journal of Abnormal and Social Psychology*, 49, 381-388.

Fiedler, F.E. (1967). *A theory of leadership effectiveness*. New York: McGraw-Hill Book Company.

Fiedler, F.E. (1973). Personality and situational determinants of leader behavior. In E.A. Fleishman and J.G. Hunt (Eds.),& *Current develoments in the study of leadership*. Carbondale, Ill.: Southern Illinois University Press.

Fleishman, E.A. (1957a). A leader behavior description for industry. In R.M. Stogdill and A.E. Coons (Eds.), *Leader behavior: Its description and measurement*. Columbus: The Ohio State University.

Fleishman, E.A. (1957b). The leadership opinion questionnaire. In R.M. Stogdill and A.E. Coons (Eds.), *Leader behavior: Its description and measurement*. Columbus: The Ohio State University.

French, J.R.P., and Raven, B. (1959). The bases of social power. In D. Cartwright (Ed.), *Studies in Social Power*. Ann Arbor, Mich.: Institute for Social Research.

Halpin, A.W., and Winer, B.J. (1957). A factorial study of the leader behavior description. In R.M. Stogdill and A.E. Coons (Eds.), *Leader behavior: Its description and measurement*. Columbus: The Ohio State University.

Heller, F.A., and Yukl, G. (1969). Participation, managerial decision-making, and situational variables. *Organizational Behavior and Human Performance*, 4, 227-234.

Hemphill, J.K., and Coons, A.E. (1957). Development of the Leader Behavior Description Questionnaire. In R.M. Stogdill and A.E. Coons (Eds.), *Leader behavior: Its description and measurement*. Columbus: The Ohis State University.

Hendry, L.B. (1968). The assessment of personality traits in the coach-swimmer relationship and a preliminary examination of the "father-figure" stereotype. *Research Quarterly*, 39, 543-551.

Hendry, L.B. (1969). A personality study of highly successful and "ideal" swimming coaches. *Research Quarterly*, 40, 299-305.

168

Hersey, P., and Blanchard, K.H. (1969). Life cycle theory of leadership. *Training and Development Journal*, May, 16-34.

Hersey, P., and Blanchard, K.H. (1977). *Management of Organizational Behavior*. Englewood Cliffs, N.J.: Prentice-Hall, Inc.

Hollander, E.P., and Julian, J.W. (1969). Contemporary trends in the analysis of leadership processes. *Psychological Bulletin, 71*, 387-397.

House, R.J. (1971). A path-goal theory of leader effectiveness. *Administrative Science Quarterly, 16*, 321-338.

House, R.J. (1977). A 1976 theory of charismatic leadership. In J.G. Hunt and L.L. Larson (Eds.), *Leadership: The cutting edge*. Carbondale, Ill.: Southern Illinois University Press.

House, R.J., and Dessler, G. (1974). The path-goal theory of leadership: Some post hoc and a priori tests. In J.G. Hunt and L.L. Larson (Eds.), *Contingency approaches to leadership*. Carbondale, Ill.: Southern Illinois University Press.

House, R.J., and Mitchell, T.R. (1974). Path-goal theory of leadership. *Journal of Contemporary Business, 3*, 81-97.

Katz, D., Maccoby, N., Gurin, G., and Floor, L. *Productivity, supervision, and morale among railroad workers*. Ann Arbor, Mich.: University of Michigan.

Katz, D., Maccoby, N., and Morse, N. (1950). *Productivity, supervision and morale in an office situation*. Ann Arbor, Mich.: University of Michigan.

Kerr, S., and Jermier, J.M. (1978). Substitutes for leadership: Their meaning and measurement. *Organizational Behavior and Human Performance, 22*, 375-403.

Larson, L.L., and Rowland, K. (1974). Leadership style and cognitive complexity. *Academy of Management Journal, 17*, 36-45.

Likert, R. (1967). *The human organization*. New York: McGraw-Hill Book Company.

Lorsch, J.W., and Morse, J.J. (1974). *Organizations and Their Members: A Contingency Approach*. New York: Harper and Row.

Maier, N.R.F. (1974). *Psychlogy in industrial organizations*. Boston: Houghton Mifflin.

McLelland, D.C. (1961). *The achieving society*. New York: Van Nostrand.

McLelland, D.C., and Burnham, D.H. (1976). Power is the great motivator. *Harvard Business Review, 54*, 100-110.

McLelland, D.C., and Winter D. (1969). *Motivating Economic Achievement*. New York: The Free Press.

McGregor, D. (1960). *The human side of enterprise*. New York: McGraw-Hill Book Company.

Morse, J.J. (1976). Person-Job Congruence and Individual Adjustment and Development. *Human Relations, 28*, 841-861.

Morse, N.C., and Reimer, E. (1956). The experimental change of a major organizational variable. *Journal of Abnormal and Social Psychology, 51*, 120-129.

Osborn, R.N., and Hunt, J.G. (1975). An adaptive-reactive theory of leadership: The role of macro variables in leadership research. In J.G. Hunt and L.L. Larson (Eds.), *Leadership frontiers*. Kent: Kent State University.

Ogilvie, B.C., and Tutko, T.A. (1966). *Problem athletes and how to handle them*. London: Pelham Books.

Sheridan, J.E., and Downey, H.K., and Slocum, J.W. (1975). Testing causal relationships of House's path-goal theory of leadership effectiveness. In J.G. Hunt and L.L. Larson(Eds.), *Leadership frontiers*. Kent: Kent State University.

Stogdill, R.M. (1963). *Manual for the Leader Behavior Description Questionnaire - Form XII*. Columbus: Ohio State University.

Szilagyi, A.D., and Wallace, M.J. (1980). *Organizational behavior and performance*. Santa Monica: Goodyear Publishing Company, Inc.

Tannenbaum, R., and Schmidt, W.H. (1973). How to choose a leadership pattern. *Harvard Business Review, 51,* 162-180.

Vroom, V.H., and Jago, A.G. (1978). On the validity of the Vroom-Yetton model. *Journal of Applied Psychology, 63,* 151-162.

Vroom, V.H., and Yetton, R.N. (1973). *Leadership and decision-making.* Pittsburgh: University of Pittsburgh Press.

Wynne, B.E., and Hunsaker, P.L. (1975). A human information-processing approach to the study of leadership. In J.G. Hunt and L.L. Larson (Eds.), *Leadership frontiers.* Kent: Kent State University.

Yukl, G.A. (1971). Toward a behavioral theory of leadership. *Organizational Behavior and Human Performance, 6,* 414-440.

Yukl, G.A. (1981). *Leadership in organizations.* Englewood Cliffs, N.J.: Prentice-Hall Inc.

CHAPTER 7

EVALUATING

As was pointed out in Chapter 1, evaluating is defined as the process of assessing the degree to which the organization as a whole and various units and individuals have accomplished what they set out to do (see Chapter 1). It was also pointed out that the four managerial functions — planning, organizing, leading, and evaluating — must be considered as ongoing processes that are intricately intertwined with each other. Thus, the planning process sets the stage for organizational initiatives while the evaluating function provides the rationale for the revision or reorganization of organizational activities. From this perspective, evaluating is very critical to the management of any organization.

Evaluating, as defined above, is a broad concept encompassing the organization as a whole, the units within it, and the members of the organization. Theorists and practitioners have traditionally distinguished between the evaluation of the organization and its units — *organizational effectiveness* — and evaluation of individual performances — *performance evaluation*. Since this text is concerned with macro issues relating to sport organizations, only the concept of organizational effectiveness is examined here.

Organizational effectiveness is, perhaps, the most controversial and complex concept in management. A review of the literature shows that a number of authors have studied organizational effectiveness from different perspectives, and using different criteria (Campbell, 1977; Steers, 1975). For example, some have used a single criterion of effectiveness while others have used multiple criteria. Some have approached the problem from a *normative* perspectives (i.e., *what ought to be*) —a perspective that simply reflects the theoretical expectations for an organization. On the other hand, some authors have taken a *descriptive* approach (i.e., *what is*).

Thus, as recent summaries of the literature suggest, the effectiveness concept has proved to be imprecise — there is no consensus on its definition, and, therefore, on its measurement (e.g., Campbell, 1977; Molnar and Rogers, 1976). It is possible, however, to reconcile the various theoretical orientations toward organizational effectiveness and produce a gestalt view of the construct. This is the approach adopted in this book.

Specifically, the four significant models of organizational effectiveness —the *goals model,* the *system resource model,* the *process model,* and the *multiple constituency model* — are examined within the general framework of a systems perspectives (Chapter 2 contains a lengthy discussion of the systems view of organizations). In order to facilitate the discussion of these four models, the input-throughput-output model of a system is reproduced in Exhibit 7.1.The exhibit also shows how the various models of effectiveness relate to the specific elements of the input-throughput-output cycle.

Exhibit 7.1. Models of Organizational Effectiveness.

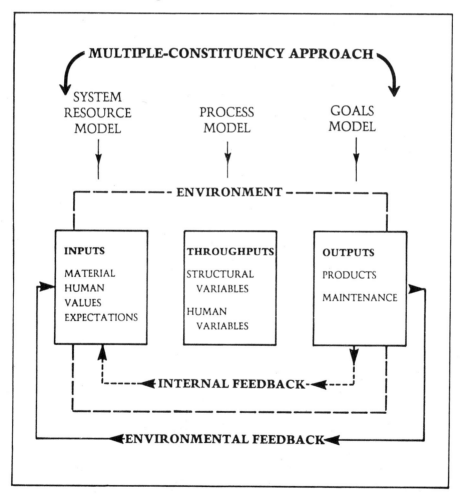

Goals Model of Organizational Effectiveness

The most fundamental approach to the study of organizational effectiveness is contained in the definition provided above. That is, effectiveness is the degree to which an organization has achieved its goals (Etzioni, 1964; Price,1972).[1] Implicit in this definition is the assumption that because organizations exist to achieve some specific purpose, an organization's effectiveness is a function of the degree to which it has achieved those goals. Thus, if a fitness firm has established that making a specific amount of profit is its goal and, then, is successful, it can be described as an effective organization. Similarly, a national sport governing body might set a goal that its national team will be ranked in the top ten in the world within a two year period. If the team is only ranked fifteenth at the end of that period, it can be considered an ineffective organization. For proponents of the goals model, the concept of effectiveness is the ultimate dependent variable (i.e., the bottom line) in any organizational analysis.

Two underlying conditions for the goals model of effectiveness become evident from the examples given above. The first is that a goal must be identifiable. In the two examples, the goals were the set amount of profit for the fitness firm, and the world ranking for the sport governing body. The second condition is that organizational performance must be clearly measurable. Thus, there is no difficulty in measuring the profit made by the fitness firm or the world ranking attained by the sport governing body. In other words, in the two examples, the criteria of effectiveness were crystallized (i.e., goals are clear and precise) and they were also observable and measurable (Hasenfeld, 1983).

While the goals model is intuitively appealing, the two conditions behind the model — *clarity of goals*, and *measurement of goal attainment* — may not be valid for all types of organizations.

Clarity of Goals

As was noted in Chapter 3, many organizations tend to proclaim their goals in broad, global terms. That is, their goals are designed to delineate a domain of

---

1. The terms *effectiveness* and *efficiency* are generally used interchangeably. However, from an organizational perspective, they are quite different. Effectiveness refers to goal attainment per se while efficiency relates to the amount of resources utilized in attaining that goal (Etzioni, 1964). An example from the athletic field serves to illustrate this distinction. A six foot tall individual might clear six feet in the high jump while a five and one-half foot tall individual might clear five feet ten inches. The taller individual is more effective because he/she cleared two inches more than the other person. However, the shorter individual is more efficient because the height cleared (goal achieved) was greater in relation to personal height (resources).A cost-benefit ratio is used by many organizations to reflect efficiency. These organizations use efficiency as measure of, not a synonym for effectiveness.

activity, and their charters and official notifications are formulated to rationalize their existence and to justify support from the larger community (Perrow, 1961). However, global statements (*official goals* in Perrow's terminology) do not provide a focus for organizational analysis. And, if you do not know where you wanted to go in the first place, how can you establish whether you have arrived?

Price (1972), while acknowledging the difficulty of identifying organizational goals, suggested that there are ways to overcome this limitation. For example, he felt that it is possible to identify the real or operative goals of the organization by focusing on the major decision makers. Their statements and their decisions regarding major organizational processes (like budgeting and staffing) should reveal the organization's priorities. He also argued that the actual activities of the organization and its members will clearly reveal what goals are sought by the organization.

Although Price's proposals have some merit, there are problems in their implementation. For example, Price's assumption that there will be consensus among the major decision-makers on the goals for an organization might not be true in all cases (Lawrence and Lorsch, 1967). Further, as was noted in Chapter 3, an organization's operative goals might not remain stable over time. Insofar as the major decision makers might have fluctuating preferences and, insofar as their power to influence decisions is subject to change (this reflects the notion of *dominance of coalitions* referred to in Chapter 3), the operative goals of an organization also might shift. Thus, it might not be possible to obtain the clarity and focus necessary to apply the goals model.

Many organizations pursue multiple goals and this factor also limits the utility of a goals model approach for the analysis of organizational effectiveness. For instance, the sport governing body of the previous example might have two goals -to increase the number of its registered clubs and to improve upon its world ranking. Prior to assessing the relative goal attainment, it would be necessary to know the relative importance attached to each.

The problem of multiple goals is further complicated by the fact that some organizational goals can be in conflict with each other (see Chapter 3). When this is the case, the attainment of one goal contributes to a failure to attain the second. That is, the organization would be effective in terms of one goal but would be ineffective in terms of the conflicting goal. For example, in the case of an intercollegiate athletic program, the goal of promoting a large number of sports and the goal of winning national championships might not be attainable simultaneously within the context of limited resources. This issue of multiple and/or conflicting goals is not addressed by the goals model.

Measurement of Goal Attainment

As indicated previously, the second assumption of the goals model is that the outcomes of the organization can be measured and compared against the priority established for the goals. But, objectively measuring outputs (i.e., goal attainment) is a problem in service organizations. For example, in many universities the "promotion of total health" is a goal of intercollegiate athletics. It should be obvious that it is not possible to validly determine the degree to which this goal is attained or approached. Similarly, the university as a whole may have as its goal, "the education of youth". Again, this goal is not easily quantifiable.[2] In short, services , in contrast to goods, are intangible, and, therefore, the quality of services cannot be easily ascertained. Thus, the problem of measuring outputs is acute in all service organizations, particularly in professional service organizations. Consequently, in these cases, the goals model appears to have little utility.

In overview, the goals model focuses on the degree to which a goal is attained as a measure of effectiveness. Consequently, it is meaningful in organizations where goals are specific and clearly articulated, where they are stable over time, and, where organizational performance can be objectively measured. Those organizations that possess these characteristics tend to adopt the goals model because it is rational. When a professional sport team fires its coach, it is usually because the organization has not achieved its goal of winning a minimum number of games. Whatever else the coach might have accomplished is irrelevant. From the organization's point of view, the bottom line on effectiveness is the win-loss ratio. It is an output that is clear and easily measurable. Many organizations, however, either do not possess the luxury of clearly defined goals, or goal attainment cannot be objectively measured. When this is the case, other models of effectiveness must be employed.

The System Resource Model of Organizational Effectiveness

An alternate model of effectiveness - *the system resource model* — focuses on the inputs of the organization (Exhibit 7.1). Yuchtman and Seashore (1967),

---

2. Some quantitative measures such as the number of graduating students and students' scores on standardized tests are often used by educational institutions as indicators of their effectiveness. As Hoy and Miskel (1982) pointed out, assessing school effectiveness through such measures is based more on expediency rather than theory. That is, such quantitative measures are readily available, and easily understood by those who demand "accountability" of the schools. Although such measures are significant by themselves, they might not indicate effectiveness in terms of educating the youth. For example, the number of students graduated might, indeed, be a reflection of lower standards. Standardized tests measuring cognitive skills are just that. They do not measure criteria in the affective domain like "motivation, creativity, self-confidence, and aspirations — all of which are needed for future success in school and adult life" (Hoy and Miskel, 1982, p. 330).

who proposed this model, defined effectiveness as "the ability of the organization, in either absolute or relative terms, to exploit its environment in the acquisition of scarce and valued resources" (p. 898). Every organization must compete with other organizations for the resources from the larger society. Thus, an effective organization is one which gains an advantageous bargaining position relative to other organizations which share the same environment.[3]

When a university assesses the relative superiority of its first year students, or the relative amount of research grants secured by its faculty, it has adopted the perspective of the system resource model. Similarly, when coaches and athletic administrators use the number and quality of athletes who tried out for the various teams and/or season tickets sold as a measure of effectiveness, they are also using a system resource approach.

It might appear at first glance that the goals model and the system resource model are significantly different — the former emphasizes the outputs of the organization while the latter emphasizes the inputs. This is not the case, however. They are integrally linked if the organization is viewed as an open system (see Exhibit 7.1). Any organization, as an open system, must be in a profitable exchange position with its environment. That is, it must be able to obtain essential inputs from the environment. But, this is only possible on a continuing basis when its outputs are acceptable to the environment. Thus, a measure of the degree to which the system is able to obtain its resources is, in fact, a measure of the acceptability and utility of its outputs. When large numbers of students wish to enroll in a particular university, it is presumed that the programs offered by that university are of high quality. Similarly, when clients select one tennis club rather than another, it is implied that the facilities and services in that club are superior. In short, the quality of the services provided by organizations is inferred from the quantity of demand for their services. These demands, in turn, translate into inputs for the organization. Thus, the system resource model quantifies one element (inputs) and uses it as a surrogate or substitute measure for another element (outputs) which is not as easily quantifiable.

Viewed from a different perspective, an *operative goal* of an organization might, indeed, be to obtain the resources from the environment. Thus, measuring the extent of resource acquisition is the equivalent of measuring goal attainment. Yuchtman and Seashore (1967) made reference to this when they noted:

> *The better the bargaining position of an organization, the more capable it is of attaining its varied and often transient goals [operative goals], and the more capable it is of allowing the attainment of personal*

---

3. The significance of the organization's bargaining position in the context of its environment was highlighted in Chapter 4. It was suggested that the members of the institutional and managerial subsystems must have the ability to influence the elements in the distal and task environments respectively.

goals of members. Processes of 'goal formation' and 'goal displacement'
in organizations are thus seen not as defining ultimate criteria of
effectiveness, but as strategies adopted by members for enhancing the
bargaining position of their organization. (p. 898)

When Yuchtman and Seashore outlined the system resource model of organizational effectiveness, they felt that it was valid and applicable to all organizations. And, it is true that the model provides a useful framework in many instances. For example, the system resource model is highly relevant for professional service organizations because their output cannot be objectively measured. Consequently, their effectiveness is best measured by the demand for their services. Similarly, the system resource model is also relevant for volunteer, non-profit organizations. Their major source of funding is from the contributions and donations of members of the larger community. Consequently, the degree to which these organizations are able to attract financial support is a measure of their effectiveness.

There is some question, however, whether public sector and third sector organizations (see Chapter 2 again) can legitimately use the system resource model. A distinguishing characteristic of these organizations is that their resources are guaranteed (to some extent at least) by a superior organization (e.g., government). In the case of publicly funded school systems, for example, children of the community must attend a specific school. And, therefore, that school is assured of a fixed sum of money for every student who attends. Under these circumstances, it would be inappropriate for the school to claim effectiveness on the basis of the number of students in attendance in the school or the total funds received from the government.

Similarly, the total funds generated by a sport governing body could ordinarily be a legitimate measure of effectiveness. However, this measure becomes meaningless if the government provides subsidies. Also, an intercollegiate athletic program cannot use the athletic fees paid by the students as a measure of effectiveness if those fees were levied and collected by the university. The student fees are a requirement of enrollment in the university; the total amount generated through the fees is a function of the total number of students in the university.

It would be legitimate, however, for the third sector organizations in the above examples to claim effectiveness on the basis of the acquisition of resources outside of government support. Thus, a sport governing body might generate a considerable amount of money through corporate sponsorships and/or private donations. It might also secure superior human resources in terms of athletes and volunteer coaches and officials. These all would be legitimate indices of effectiveness.

In overview, the system resource model contains the supposition that the degree to which an organization can influence environmental elements and secure necessary resources is a measure of its effectiveness. This emphasis on the input phase is meaningful only to the extent that the organization's outputs cannot be easily be measured and/or its resources are not assured through legislative authority.

The Process Model of Organizational Effectiveness

If an organization cannot use the goals model because it cannot objectively measure its outputs, and if it cannot use the system resource model because its resources are underwritten by government regulations, how can it evaluate effectiveness? A number of authors (e.g., Pfeffer, 1977; Steers, 1977) have suggested that, as a partial solution, the focus should be directed toward the internal *processes* of the organization rather than on its proposed end states. From a systems perspective, this involves an emphasis on the throughputs which links the inputs to outputs (see Exhibit 7.1).

The underlying rationale for the process model of effectiveness is that the conversion of the inputs into acceptable outputs is based on the throughput processes adopted by the organization. And, if those throughput processes are internally logical, consistent, and without friction, then it can be assumed that the organization is effective. Further, as Mott (1972) pointed out, organizational processes are expected to be *adaptable* to changes in the environment, and *flexible* to accomodate fluctuating workloads. That is, the organization is doing what is rational in the context of its goals and its environment.

The process model can be illustrated by a school system which has as its purpose, the education of youth. As noted before, neither the goals nor the system resource model can be validly used in the assessment of the school system's effectiveness. The most crucial processes within the school system are the efforts that have gone into the design of the curriculum, the logical progression within the total curriculum, and the teaching and evaluation methods employed. An evaluation of these processes would be one measure of the relative effectiveness of the school system. Another measure would be the general policies and procedures, the satisfaction expressed by both teachers and students, and the lack of conflict within the school.

As was the case with the goals and system resource models, the process model of effectiveness has some advantages. But, the evaluation of internal processes also poses problems. The process model presupposes that a body of experts can judge the appropriateness of specific processes. And, because experts' judgements are accepted as correct, there is a tendency to specify the "appropriate" processes and procedures in advance for all schools to follow.

When this happens, every school or school system must be judged as effective if they followed the specified processes.

This trend is evident in third sector organizations which depend heavily on the government for financial support. For example, many governments offer financial assistance to sport governing bodies for specific programs. These programs are assumed to lead to better management of the sport governing bodies, better recruitment and training of the national team, and, so on. The sport governing bodies, in turn, must follow these guidelines and institute the suggested programs in order to receive the government grants. Thus, all sport governing bodies tend to become identical in terms of their internal processes.

Weber's concept of a bureaucracy is another instance where the problems associated with the use of internal processes is highlighted. Weber's bureaucratic prescriptions are normative in the sense that they suggest that all organizations must be bureaucratized in order to be efficient (see Chapter 4). However, the best judgement that can be made about organizations using the process model is whether an organization is more or less bureaucratized: But, to relate the degree of bureaucratization to effectiveness would be inappropriate.

Thus, the danger in the use of the process model of effectiveness is that organizations would tend to deify the processes irrespective of their relationship to effectiveness. An emphasis on processes could be counterproductive from a systems perspective. The concept of equifinality (see Chapter 2) suggests that two organizations adopting two different sets of processes could both be equally effective. Consequently, it would be inappropriate to judge them as effective or ineffective on the basis of their internal processes.

In overview, the process model of effectiveness emphasizes the significance of the throughput processes which link the inputs and outputs of an organization and the need for the internal throughput processes to be congruent and goal directed. If these processes are internally consistent and goal directed, they are considered to contribute to goal attainment. As a consequence, they also can be used as indicators of organizational effectiveness. But, when specific processes are designated as most effective, there is a strong likelihood that uniform procedural prescriptions will be set out for all organizations.

The Multiple-Constituency Model of Effectiveness

Connolly, Conlon, and Deutsch (1980) have criticized both the goals and system resource models of effectiveness for their assumption that "it is possible, and desirable, to arrive at a single set of evaluative criteria, and thus at a single statement of organizational effectiveness" (p. 212). Instead, they proposed:

> a view of organizational effectiveness in which several (potentially, many) different effectiveness statements can be made about the focal organization, reflecting the criterion sets of different individuals and groups we shall refer to as 'constituencies'. (Connolly et al., 1980, p. 212)

The constituencies they refer to are the owners, managers, employees, clients, suppliers, and other "stake holders". The constituent groups may be within the organization (e.g., senior administrators, employee groups), or they may belong to the environment (e.g., consumer groups, suppliers). In the case of a faculty of physical education, the students, the faculty, the staff, and the dean and other administrative heads would form the internal constituencies. The external constituencies would include the university administrators, the senate, and other faculties.

Connolly et al., noting that it was "somewhat arbitrary to label one of these perspectives a priori as the 'correct' one" (p. 212), suggested that effectiveness must be considered as a plural concept — it is *effectivenessess* that should be considered, not *effectiveness*.

It is important to distinguish between a multidimensional approach to effectiveness and the multiple-constituency approach. The former approach simply suggests that an organization should be evaluated on different dimensions — resource acquisition, productivity, smooth functioning of internal processes, and so on (Evan 1976; Steers, 1975).[4] In the multiple-constituency model, however, a focal organization is evaluated by the various

---

4. Evan (1976) suggested that "to appraise the effectiveness of an organization with the aid of systems theory ... one must measure its performance with respect to all four systemic processes as well as their interrelationships" (p. 19). The four systemic processes that Evan referred to are the inputs, throughputs, outputs, and feedback of a system (see Exhibit 7.1 again). Evan also proposed a sample set of systemic indicators of effectiveness for various types of organizations. For example, he suggested that colleges and universities could use the number of students who graduate (output), the annual budget (input), and the cost of the information system (throughput) as effectiveness indicators. Also, it may be necessary for some organizations to measure effectiveness at different points in the input-throughput-output cycle since no (or only few) output measure may be available or feasible. For example, Szyszlo (1984) found that administrators of Canadian sport governing bodies endorsed a goals model approach for evaluating their elite sport programs. However, this approach was rejected for the evaluation of mass sport programs. This, of course, reflects the fact that an objective measure for the goal attainment of an elite program is readily available (i.e., the performance record of the national team in international competitions). However, an objective measure is not available for mass sport programs. It was also pointed out above that third sector organizations should not use the securing of monetary resources as a measure of effectiveness — governments contribute most of the financial resources and, therefore, finances lose their potency as an effectiveness indicator. Consistent with this perspective, Szyszlo found that sport administrators did, in fact, emphasize the importance of the input of human resources to a greater extent than the input of monetary resources as effectiveness indicators of both the elite and mass sport programs. Finally, the administrators in Szyszlo's study endorsed the process model of effectiveness for the evaluation of both elite and mass programs. In essence, they took a multidimensional approach to evaluating sport governing bodies.

groups on the same dimensions. For example, the national team preparations of a sport governing body might be evaluated differently by the athletes, the clubs, and the administrators. Thus, the multiple-constituency approach focuses on *who* should evaluate rather than on *what* should be evaluated. From this perspective, the multiple-constituency approach subsumes all other models of effectiveness as illustrated in Exhibit 7.1.

Connolly et al. pointed out that the multiple-constituency approach to effectiveness incorporates the notion that different goals will be held by different groups in an organization. It was pointed out in Chapter 3 that organizations solve this problem by stating their goals — the *official* goals of an organization — in more global and ambiguous terms. Global statements do not preclude different individuals or groups from holding a somewhat different perspective on the goals of the organization. Insofar as differences in the perception of goals exist, there will also be differences in the perception of organizational effectiveness.

For example, the global goal for an intercollegiate athletic program might be "the pursuit of excellence". Two different interest groups within that intercollegiate program could hold different aspirations for the program. One interest group might insist that all sports should be treated equally in terms of promotion, budget, facility allocation, and so on. The other interest group might insist that selected sports should be given preferential treatment because of their superior entertainment value. Although the official goal statement — "pursuit of excellence" -could be subscribed to equally by both interest groups, the way they would evaluate the program would be dramatically different.

In many organizations, one group may have the power over another and, therefore, its views will prevail. In fact, Pennings and Goodman (1977) proposed that effectiveness should be viewed from the perspective of the "dominant coalition" (see Chapter 3). Similarly, in some organizations, the orientations of the major decision makers (irrespective of other groups) will be the basis for judgements about effectiveness (Price, 1972). According to Connolly et al., these cases can be subsumed within the multiple-constituency approach to effectiveness." The multiple-constituency view of organizational effectiveness may be seen as embracing as special cases several existing views of the effectiveness concept" (Connolly et al., 1980, p. 213).

Although Connolly et al. emphasized the flexibility of the model — flexibility in terms of accommodating changes in the power structure among the constituencies over time — they did not clarify how the differing evaluations (by the constituencies) could be used by an organization to improve its performance. A practical application of the model would be for key decision makers of an organization to periodically gather evaluations of the organization from different constituencies. This was the approach suggested by Chelladurai, Haggerty, Campbell, and Wall (1981) and Chelladurai, Inglis, and Danylchuk (1984) for intercollegiate athletic programs. It should be apparent, however, that the responsibility for using these evaluations and deciding on the appropriate courses of action still resides with the key decision makers.

An Overview of Organizational Effectiveness

It was noted at the beginning of the chapter that the various models of effectiveness can be synthesized into a gestalt view of effectiveness. As Yuchtman and Seashore (1967) pointed out, since the three processes of an open system — acquisition of resources, transformation of the inputs (throughputs), and disposal of the outputs — are integrally linked to each other, the effectiveness of the system can be measured at any point in the input-throughput-output cycle. This is highlighted by the fact that each model of effectiveness focuses on one of the elements in the cycle (see Exhibit 7.1).

A careful examination of these four models shows that all of them do, in fact, have goal attainment as the primary concern in the assessment of effectiveness. For example, the underlying assumption of the systems resources model is that the ability of the organization to secure resources is a reflection of the environment's acceptance of the organization's outputs. Thus, the degree to which the organization secures its resources is a reflection of its goal attainment. Similarly, the process model of effectiveness links the organizational processes to the outputs of the organization. Finally, the multiple-constituency approach also emphasizes the operative goals held by different groups. The degree to which the organization has achieved the goals of the various constituencies is a measure of its effectiveness.

In overview, all models of effectiveness utilize either direct or surrogate measures of goal attainment. Therefore, the goals model should be used in those cases where goals are clear and their attainment is measurable. In those cases where specific goals cannot be identified and/or cannot be measured, the practical solution is to adopt the system resource model because there is a direct link between resource acquisition and output acceptance. The process model of effectiveness should be considered only if the former two models cannot be profitably used. Even then, care must be taken to ensure that undue emphasis is not placed on predetermined processes. In short, in choosing the criteria of effectiveness for their organizations, managers should be concerned with what Campbell (1976) calls *closeness to the final payoff*. That is, a criterion that is more closely related to the goal should be selected over those more remotely connected.

A final comment is appropriate on the concept of objectivity versus subjectivity in the assessment of organizational effectiveness. Campbell (1976) pointed out that "there is no algorithm of science that will specify which variables should be labelled as criteria of organizational effectiveness. That begins as a value judgement and ends as a political decision" (p. 40). Values held by key decision makers and their judgements about effectiveness are related to operative goals which were, in the first place, subjective. This is reality, but, what is needed is the realization that all the objective computations and calculations cannot mask this fact.

Summary

Various models of effectiveness —goals, system resource, process, and multiple constituencies models — were shown to be related to the systems view of organizations. It was emphasized that all models are goal oriented but the difficulty encountered in the measurement of goal attainment leads to a focus on different surrogate measures. The organizational conditions under which each model would be appropriate were also discussed. Finally, it was suggested that the selection of effectiveness criteria must be based on the degree to which they reflect the ultimate criterion — the attainment of goals.

Questions for Discussion

1. Select a sport organization. What criteria would you use to evaluate its effectiveness? Why?

2. Give examples of sport organizations where each of the four models of effectiveness — goals, system resource, process, and multiple constituency models — would be appropriate.

3. List as many criteria of effectiveness as possible for a sport organization. Place them on Campbell's (1976) continuum of *closeness to the final payoff.*

4. According to your perceptions, what are the effectiveness criteria used in evaluating your faculty or department? Who decides on these criteria? Can you infer their operative goals from these criteria?

References

Chelladurai, P., Haggerty, T.R., Campbell, L., and Wall, S. (1981). A factor analytic study of effectiveness criteria in intercollegiate athletics. *Canadian Journal of Applied Sport Sciences, 6,* 81-86.

Chelladurai, P., Inglis, S.E., and Danylchuk, K.E. (1984). Priorities in intercollegiate athletics: Development of a scale. *Research Quarterly for Exercise and Sport, 55,* 74-79.

Campbell, J.P. (1976). Contributions research can make in understanding organizational effectiveness. In L.S. Spray (Ed.), *Organizational effectiveness: Theory - research -utilization.* Kent, Ohio: Graduate School of Business Administration, Kent State University.

Campbell, J.P. (1977). On the nature of organizational effectiveness. In P.S. Goodman and J.M. Pennings (Eds.), *New perspectives on organizational effectiveness.* San Francisco: Jossey-Bass.

Connolly, T., Conlon, E.J., Deutsch, S.J. (1980). Organizational effectiveness: A multiple-constituency approach. *Academy of Management Review, 5,* 211-217.

Evan, W.M. (1976). Organization theory and organizational effectiveness: An exploratory analysis. In L.S. Spray(Ed.), *Organizational effectiveness: Theory - research -utilization.* Kent, Ohio: Graduate School of Business Administration, Kent State University.

Etzioni, A. (1964). *Modern organizations.* Englewood Cliffs, N.J.: Prentice-Hall, Inc.

Hasenfeld, Y. (1983). *Human service organizations.* Englewood Cliffs, N.J.: Prentice-Hall, Inc.

Hoy. W.K., and Miskel, C.G. (1982). *Educational Administration: Theory, research, and practice.* New York: Random House.

Lawrence, P.R., and Lorsch, J.W. (1967). *Organization and environment: Managing differentiation and integration.* Cambridge, Mass.: Harvard Graduate School of Business Administration.

Molnar, J.J., and Rogers, D.L. (1976). Organizational effectiveness: An empirical comparison of the goal and system resource approaches. *Sociological Quarterly, 17,* 401-413.

Mott, P.E. (1972). *The characteristics of effective organizations.* New York: Harper & Row.

Pennings, J.M., and Goodman, P.S. (1977). Toward a workable framework. In P.S. Goodman and J.M. Pennings (Eds.), *New perspectives on organizational effectiveness.* San Francisco: Jossey-Bass.

Perrow, C. (1961). The analysis of goals in complex organizations. *American Sociological Review, 26,* 854-866.

Pfeffer, J. (1977). Usefulness of the concept. In P.S. Goodman and J.M. Pennings (Eds.), *New perspectives on organizational effectiveness.* San Francisco: Jossey-Bass.

Price, J.L. (1972). The study of organizational effectiveness. *Sociological Quarterly, 13,* 3-15.

Steers, R.M. (1975). Problems in the measurement of organizational effectiveness. *Administrative Science Quarterly, 20,* 546-558.

Steers, R.M. (1977). *Organizational effectiveness: A behavioral view.* Pacific Palisades, Cal.: Goodyear Publishing Company, Inc.

Szyszlo, M.J.D. (1984). *A model of effectiveness for national sport governing bodies: Perceptions of their administrators.* Unpublished master's thesis. University of Western Ontario, London.

Yuchtman, E., and Seashore, S.E. (1967). A system resource approach to organizational effectiveness. *American Sociological Review, 32,* 891-903.

Index (Subject)

Index (Author)